THE TEN-KEY TOUCH SYSTEM ON MODERN CALCULATORS

A STEP-BY-STEP APPROACH

By
Gilbert Eckern
and
Walt Hardin

Star

PUBLISHING COMPANY

PUBLISHING COMPANY
P.O. Box 68
Belmont, California 94002
(415) 591-3505

Gilbert Eckern
Professor Emeritus
American River College
Sacramento, California

Walt Hardin
Professor of Business
American River College
Sacramento, California

> *This book is dedicated to our wives,*
> *Harriet Eckern and Nadine Hardin,*
> *in recognition of their encouragement*
> *and support in the development of this*
> *text.*

Previous Edition Titled: The Ten-Key Touch System on Electronic Calculators
With Business and Industry Applications

Managing Editor: Stuart Hoffman

Typesetting: Beverly Page

Layout and Graphics: Douglas B. Hurd

Printed in U.S.A.

ISBN: 0-89863-132-7

REVISED PRINTING
9 8 7 6 5 4

TABLE OF CONTENTS

PREFACE

In the United States, more people earn their living in office occupations than in any other type of employment. The modern electronic office calculator is one of the most important office tools — proficiency on the calculator is, therefore, an important skill.

Ten-key calculator skills are an important advantage to secretaries, bookkeepers, and accountants with their frequent use of numbers — and to other business professionals, executives and engineers too, who will find the "ten-key pad" part of the computer that is commonplace in both large and small businesses.

Individualization of learning and instruction is built right into the structure of the book. Step-by-step layouts guide students through example problems on the calculator and help reinforce learning.

Above all else, productivity in calculating is determined by speed and accuracy. Through speed drills and accuracy drills the student builds confidence and competence, rapidly gaining speed and accuracy. A wide variety of practical applications helps put this skill to work, unifying mathematical concepts with touch control mastery.

THE TEN-KEY TOUCH CONTROL SYSTEM ON MODERN CALCULATORS, and its approach are easily adapted to the particular machines on your campus or office.

We would like to thank the various calculator manufacturers for their help in preparing this text workbook.

Gilbert Eckern
Walt Hardin

A NOTE FROM THE AUTHORS AND PUBLISHER

Any brand or model of electronic calculator may be used with this book.

GENERAL OBJECTIVES

1. Create an overall appreciation for the purpose of business calculating machines in business and industry.

2. Show an awareness of the importance of learning to operate business calculating machines by developing saleable skills.

3. Emphasize the importance of the 10-key touch control system in developing speed and accuracy.

4. Demonstrate a problem-solving attitude for the computational skills involved by the execution of each area of the instructional objectives.

5. Develop a skill with the logical reasoning method of flowcharting with the calculator.

6. Integrate mathematical skills with computational skills while solving the practice problems.

7. Create an overall awareness of the need for speed and accuracy as it applies to business and industry performance.

8. Develop industriousness, punctuality, and self-discipline by completing objectives as scheduled, and working independently on business machine calculation problems.

9. Develop a basic understanding of the terminology, concepts, and procedures which are relevant to business and industry.

10. Develop fundamental skills in problem solving situations: organizing, analyzing, synthesizing, recording, and reporting business related problems.

BUSINESS MATHEMATICS REVIEW

READING NUMBERS

The most important part of any number is the *decimal point*. Every number is written around a decimal point. Whole units are located to the left of it, and anything less than a whole unit is located to the right of it. The decimal point may be considered as a point of reference, identifying each digit by its relative position. For example, the following number (1,534.367) is read: one thousand, five hundred thirty-four and three hundred sixty-seven thousandths. This means there are 1,534 whole units, plus $\frac{367}{1000}$ of one unit.

The following are examples of numbers and how they are read:

12,978,543.896	— Twelve million, nine hundred seventy-eight thousand, five hundred forty-three and eight hundred ninety-six thousandths.
1,423,601.78	— One million, four hundred twenty-three thousand, six hundred one and seventy-eight hundredths.
670,809.9	— Six hundred seventy thousand, eight hundred nine and nine tenths.
56,206	— Fifty-six thousand, two hundred six.
7,000	— Seven thousand.
3,980	— Three thousand, nine hundred eighty.

ADDITION

Addition is the process of combining two or more numbers so as to obtain a number called *their sum* or *total*.

The numbers being added are *Addends*.

The result is the *Sum*.

43.89	Addend
17.98	Addend
61.87	Sum

To prove the accuracy of your addition, you merely reverse the order and add again.

SUBTRACTION

Subtraction is the process of finding the difference between two numbers.

The number from which another is to be subtracted is the *Minuend*.

The number to be subtracted from another is the *Subtrahend*.

The result is the *Difference* (or *Remainder*).

890	Minuend
−78	Subtrahend
812	Difference (or Remainder)

To prove the accuracy of your subtraction, you add the *Difference* to your *Subtrahend* and the result should be the same as your *Minuend*.

CREDIT OR NEGATIVE BALANCE

When subtracting a larger number from a smaller number, the result is called a *Credit* or *Negative Balance*.

1.25
−2.50
−1.25 (Credit Balance)

MULTIPLICATION

Multiplication is repeated addition.

The number to be multiplied is the *Multiplicand*.

The number by which another is multiplied is the *Multiplier*.

The result of the multiplication is the *Product*.

1245	Multiplicand
× 19	Multiplier
23655	Product

Although the multiplicand and multiplier are interchangeable, the product is always the same. If one number is larger than the other, the larger number is usually used as the multiplicand.

DIVISION

Division is repeated subtraction.

The number to be divided by another is the *Dividend*.
The number by which another is divided is the *Divisor*.
The result of the division is the *Quotient*.
Any part of the dividend left over when the quotient is not exact is the *Remainder*.

QUOTIENT ⟶ (13,75) ⟵ REMAINDER

DIVISOR ⟶ (4) / (55) ⟵ DIVIDEND

Quotient $13\frac{3}{4}$ Remainder

Divisor $4\overline{)55}$ Dividend

DECIMALS

Decimals are another way of expressing parts of a whole. Any proper fraction can be converted to its Decimal Equivalent by dividing the numerator by the denominator and then writing the quotient in decimal form.

$$\frac{2}{3} = 3\overline{)2.0000}^{.6667}$$ Decimal Equivalent of $\frac{2}{3}$

Reading Decimals

First decimal place	Tenths	.7	7/10
Second decimal place	Hundredths	.07	7/100
Third decimal place	Thousandths	.007	7/1000
Fourth decimal place	Ten Thousandths	.0007	7/10000
Fifth decimal place	Hundred Thousandths	.00007	7/100000

Read the number to the right of the decimal point as a whole number and give it the name of the last decimal place.

The number .489 is read as four hundred eighty-nine thousandths.

MULTIPLICATION OF DECIMALS

The multiplication of decimals is the same as the multiplication of whole numbers, except that care must be taken in placing the decimal point in the answer. The decimal point in the product has as many places as the sum of the places in the multiplicand and the multiplier:

Example:

Multiplicand	5.36	(2 places)
Multiplier	× 6.2	(1 place)
	1 072	
	32 16	
Product	33.232	(decimal point is 3 places)

Example:

Multiplicand	.218 (3 places)
Multiplier	× .31 (2 places)
	218
	654
Product	.06758 (decimal point is 5 places)

DIVISION OF DECIMALS

To divide a decimal by a whole number, place the decimal point in the quotient directly above the decimal point in the dividend and proceed as with whole numbers.

To divide a decimal by a decimal, move the decimal point in the divisor to the right until it becomes a whole number. Then move the decimal point in the dividend the same number of places to the right. (Add zeros if necessary.) Then place the decimal point in the quotient directly above the decimal point in the dividend.

$$5.6. \overline{)19.4.88} \quad \frac{3.48}{}$$

To divide a smaller dividend by a larger divisor or to extend a quotient to a given number of decimal places, add enough zeros to the right of the dividend until the dividend contains the desired number of decimal places.

$$8\overline{)2.00} \quad \frac{.25}{} \qquad 12\overline{)145.000} \quad \frac{12.083}{}$$

Answer rounded to nearest hundredth (12.08)

As a rule, carry out the division problem one more decimal place than is needed, before rounding off. If the last figure is 5 or more, drop it and add 1 to the figure in the preceding place. If the last figure is less than 5, just drop it entirely (as above).

PERCENT/DECIMALS

Percent is a commonly used term, particularly in business and finance. Some examples would be: 5% sales tax, 5% interest, etc. The word *percent* simply means *part of one hundred.*

The numbers .75, $\frac{75}{100}$, and 75% all have the same value...75 parts of 100.

To convert a decimal to a percent move the decimal two places to the right and add a percent sign (%).

Example: .25 = .25. = 25%   1.357 = 1.35.7 = 135.7%

To convert a percent to a decimal move the decimal two places to the left and drop the percent sign.

Example: 25% = .25. = .25   15.26% = .15.26 = .1526

FRACTIONS

A fraction is a number that is less than a whole number $\left(\frac{1}{2}\right)$.

The number below the line is the *Denominator* and indicates the complete number of equal parts into which the whole quantity has now been subdivided.

The number above the line is the *Numerator* and indicates how many of these equal parts are being considered.

The line dividing the two numbers means *divided by*. $\frac{Numerator}{Denominator}$

Common fractions may appear in various forms such as proper or improper.

Proper fractions, such as $\frac{1}{2}$, $\frac{1}{4}$, and $\frac{2}{2}$ are called *proper* fractions because their value is less than one.

Improper fractions, like $\frac{3}{2}$, $\frac{8}{3}$, and $\frac{17}{3}$ consist of a numerator larger than the denominator and are generally reduced to mixed numbers, such as $\frac{3}{2} = 1\frac{1}{2}$.

PERCENTAGE

Percentage is made up of three different factors: *Base, Rate,* and *Percentage.*

BASE   =   Any whole unit, for example, a person's annual income or anything you can think of as a single total unit would be considered as a base amount.

RATE   =   A part of a whole unit (base) in terms of hundredths or percent (%).

PERCENTAGE   =   A part of a whole unit (base) expressed in terms of however the base is measured. For example, if the base is measured in dollars the percentage would be expressed in dollars.

Each of these factors has its own equation.

Base	=	Percentage ÷ Rate
Percentage	=	Base × Rate
Rate	=	Percentage ÷ Base

A unique way of remembering the three equations is to think of "Pretty Blue Ribbon," then draw a circle and place the first letter of each of the words as follows:

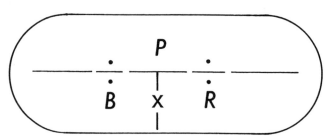

    To find the unknown factor cover the letter that represents that factor and now you have the equation, for example:

To find the Percentage, cover the letter P — that leaves B × R.

To find the Base, cover the letter B — that leaves $\frac{P}{R}$ *or* (P ÷ R).

To find the Rate, cover the letter R — that leaves $\frac{P}{B}$ *or* (P ÷ B).

COMPLEMENTS

The *Complement* of a number is the difference between that number and the next higher power of 10. For example, the complement of 8 is 2 (10 − 8). The complement of 35 is 65 (100 − 35). The complement of 400 is 600 (1000 − 400).

    Complements are used to simplify some arithmetic problems by eliminating one or more steps.

    A *Complementary Percentage* is the difference between a percent and 100%. For example, the complementary percentage of 25% is 75%.

    Complementary percentages are widely used in business where discounts or commissions are involved.

WELCOME TO THE WORLD OF BUSINESS!

You may be fast, slow, or an average learner, but one thing is certain: your attitude as much as your ability can change you from one kind of learner (or employee) to another. Approach each lesson with the attitude that good accomplishment is satisfying; learning something new is rewarding and developing a technical skill is fun. Check your attitude regularly, think back to your last lesson—did it drag or were you surprised when the class was over? Penetrate each lesson as far as you can, and make each lesson an enjoyable learning experience.

INSTRUCTIONAL OBJECTIVES

1. Develop the ten-key touch method of keyboard input on the electronic calculator through practice problems.
2. Demonstrate a high performance level of skill on addition and subtraction problems through a criterion referenced evaluation.
3. Perform multiplication problems through practice problems and criterion referenced evaluations.
4. Exhibit division capabilities of the electronic calculator through practice problems and criterion referenced evaluations.
5. Develop a competency in using the memory and constant units of the electronic calculator through practice of business and industrial applications.
6. Develop the skill of decimal placement to problems.
7. Demonstrate the skills attained from the four mathematical functions as applied to business and industrial problems.

INTRODUCTION

A calculator is designed to accomplish the four (4) functions of arithmetic: addition, subtraction, multiplication, and division. Learning to use the electronic calculator means saving time and increasing your accuracy when doing problems which were difficult to solve with pencil and paper.

The electronic calculator can be used as a tool in solving a mathematical problem in the classroom, providing you know the method. It can be used to check your work. It will give you answers to problems you know how to solve and eliminate the large amount of pencil and paper work.

In order to take advantage of the present trend of business, the student must qualify himself or herself to handle figurework swiftly and accurately. Business and technical careers now require individuals who are thoroughly trained in the technique of handling business applications with the electronic calculator.

BASIC FEATURES OF THE ELECTRONIC CALCULATOR

UNIT 1

FUNCTIONS OF THE ELECTRONIC CALCULATOR

Although there are many different models of electronic calculators, their operation is fundamentally the same. Check to see where the operating controls are on your machine. We have listed the following operating keys and their functions, as commonly found on most calculators.

If you find that there are keys on your calculator that have not been mentioned here, the operating manual for your calculator will have an explanation of those keys.

Photos Courtesy Of Canon U.S.A. Inc

Function Keys	Examples Of Keys Found On Different Calculators	Explanation
ON/OFF KEY	ON/OFF	Turns power on and off. When off, all registers (and memory) are cleared.
NUMBER KEYS	7 8 9 / 4 5 6 / 1 2 3 / 0 00 •	Enters numbers into machine.
CLEAR ENTRY KEY	C CE CL CA	This key will clear the number just entered or all entries except those in memory.
DECIMAL KEY	•	Allows for the proper placement of a decimal point when entering numbers.
ADDITION KEY	+ ±	Performs addition, repeat addition, and incremental item count.
SUBTRACTION KEY	− −=	Performs subtraction, repeat subtraction, credit balance, and incremental item count.
SUBTOTAL KEY	◇ ◇=	Prints value shown in display but does not clear the contents of the accumulator.
TOTAL KEY	* *=	Prints value shown in display and clears the contents of the accumulator.
MULTIPLICATION KEY	X	Performs multiplication, automatic constant multiplication, and intermediate sequential operations.
DIVISION KEY	÷	Performs division, automatic constant division, intermediate sequential operations.

Function Keys	Examples Of Keys Found On Different Calculators	Explanation
EQUALS KEY	`=` `*=`	Completes a multiplication or division sequence. The result may be used for further use. `*=` Acts as clear key when depressed a second time.
EQUALS PLUS KEY	`= +`	Completes a multiplication or division sequence and adds the result to accumulator.
EQUALS MINUS KEY	`= –`	Completes a multiplication or division sequence and subtracts result from the accumulator.
MEMORY PLUS KEY	`M +` `= +` `M =` `AM` `+I`	This dual function key adds previous entry directly to memory. It also completes a multiplication or division sequence and adds the result to memory.
MEMORY MINUS KEY	`M –` `= –` `–I` `M =`	This dual function key subtracts previous entry directly from memory. It also completes a multiplication or division sequence and subtracts the result from memory.
MEMORY SUBTOTAL KEY	`M◇` `MS` `S` `◇I`	Prints/displays but does not clear the contents of the memory.
MEMORY TOTAL KEY	`M*` `T` `*I`	Prints/displays and clears the contents of the memory.

SPECIAL FEATURE KEYS

Function Keys	Examples Of Keys Found On Different Calculators	Explanation
PERCENT KEY	`%` `% ±`	Used in conjunction with the Multiplication or Division key to automatically convert a number to a percent and complete a percentage calculation.
DELTA PERCENT KEY	`Δ%`	Used for obtaining increased/decreased ratios.
MARK UP, MARK DOWN KEY	`MU`	Used for performing mark up and mark down calculations.
CONSTANT KEY	`K`	Used for performing multiplication and division by a constant.
NON-ADD/DATE KEY	`#/D` `#`	This multiple function key will print entries for reference on left side of tape without affecting calculations. Will print dates and numbers.
PAPER ADVANCE KEY	`↑`	Depressing this key advances the paper tape.
DECIMAL SELECTOR	`F0234A3AM` `F643210+1+2` `012346F` `+012346F`	Allows the calculator to be set so answers will have the desired number of decimal places. The F setting allows for the maximum number of decimal places.

Function Keys	Examples Of Keys Found On Different Calculators	Explanation
ROUND-OFF SWITCH	$\boxed{\downarrow\ 5/4\ \uparrow}$	Allows you to adjust the rounding off setting.
		$\mathbf{\downarrow}$: Round down (eliminates any fractional component of a whole number).
		$5\sqrt{4}$: The last printed digit is rounded up if the first digit after the decimal control setting is 5 or more.
		$\mathbf{\uparrow}$: Round up (rounds up to the next whole number if any decimal digits exist beyond the decimal setting).
ITEM COUNT SWITCH	$\boxed{\text{OFF} \mid \text{N}+ \mid \text{N}\pm \mid \text{AVE}}$	$\blacktriangledown$: Off.
	$\boxed{\blacktriangledown \mid 1\ \text{C}+ \mid 1\text{C}\pm}\quad\boxed{\text{N}}$	IC+: The total number of added and subtracted values is registered.
		IC±: The operation of the Plus key adds to the counter; the operation of the Minus key subtracts from the counter.
PRINT SELECTOR	$\boxed{\text{NP} \mid \text{P}}\quad\boxed{\blacksquare \mid \text{P}}$ $\boxed{\text{OFF} \mid \text{PRINT} \mid \text{PAIR}}$	Print selector activates the printer and display. Nonprint position activates the display only.

TEN-KEY
TOUCH SYSTEM

INTRODUCTION TO TEN-KEY TOUCH OPERATION

Lesson Features

- Operating Parts (see pp. 6−8)
- Machine Position
- Home Keys
- Indexing Numbers

- Touch Operation
- Body and Hand Position
- Totals

Machine Position

Place your machine on the desk so that it is in a direct line with the natural curvature of your arm. Although you may not be able to have your machine in this position in your office, it is the most natural position for training purposes.

To determine how far back on the desk the machine should be, place the right elbow on the edge of the desk, with fingers slightly curved. Lower hand until fingers rest on "home" keys 4, 5, and 6.

The "Home Keys"

The keyboard is operated by the first three fingers and thumb of the right hand. The "home keys" are the starting position for touch operating any key from 1 to 9. Zero key is operated with thumb.

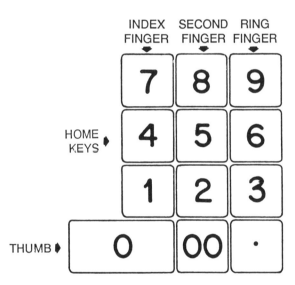

"Indexing" Numbers

To index a number means to enter the number on the keyboard. "Index" and "Enter" are terms used interchangeably in business offices.

Touch Operation

In touch operation you do not watch the machine or fingers. Keep your eyes on the work or problem at all times. Form this habit early and machine operation will become fast, easy and accurate. To help you learn the touch operation, the curvature of the home keys (4, 5, 6) is different on some machines. Touch them and feel the difference.

BODY AND HAND POSITION

A. Correct Body Position

1. Place the Operator's Manual to the left of the machine.
2. Sit erect in your chair and lean slightly forward. Your chair should be high enough so that you can place your hand over the machine keyboard with a straight wrist and without an unusual arm position.

B. Correct Hand and Arm Position

1. Clinch your fingers lightly into a fist and place your hand over the keyboard. Your wrist should be level and the line from your elbow should be in the same direction as the machine.
2. The middle row of keys (4–5–6) are considered the home row. Hold your lightly clinched hand one inch above the home row. Open your fingers into a curved position and place them lightly on the home-row keys. The first finger is placed on the 4-key, the second finger on the 5-key, and third finger on the 6-key.
3. The fingers should now be curved into a "scratching" position so that you can reach to the upper and lower row of keys without moving your hand or arm.

C. Correct Key Stroke

1. The key stroke should be fast and short. If you feel the key hit bottom, you are pushing the key too hard and taking too much time.

2. The stroke to a key above or below the home row is not completed until your finger has returned to its home row position. For example, to depress the 8-key, move the second finger to the north by itself, depress the 8-key, and return the finger immediately to its position above the 5-key. By quickly returning to the home row position, you will always know where your fingers are and will not have to look at the keyboard.

3. Keys on the keyboard are depressed in the following manner:

    a. The first finger depresses the 1, 4, and 7-keys.
    b. The second finger depresses the 2, 5, and 8-keys.
    c. The third finger depresses the 3, 6, and 9-keys.
    d. The little finger depresses the plus key.
    e. The thumb depresses the zero key.

4. Use the 5-key as your control point for touch operation.

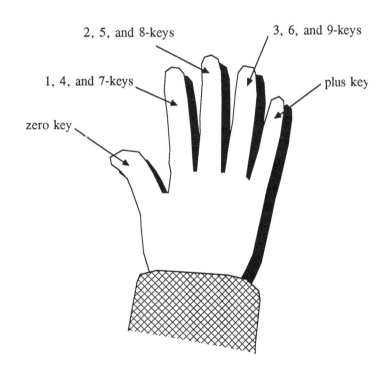

2, 5, and 8-keys   3, 6, and 9-keys

1, 4, and 7-keys   plus key

zero key

BODY AND HAND POSITION

Set Decimal Selector at 0
The 4-, 5-, 6-Keys (Home Keys)

Use first finger on 4-key — middle finger on 5-key — ring finger on 6-key. The first number of the first problem below is 456. Index the 4-key, then the 5-key and 6-key in that order, using the proper fingers. After indexing the number on the keyboard, touch the Plus key with the little finger to enter the number. Continue indexing and entering each number in the column by depressing the Plus key. After indexing the last number, depress the TOTAL KEY.

PRACTICE PROBLEMS
Work each problem a minimum of 5 times

456	645	445	544	546	456	644	654	645
444	555	455	554	465	444	645	446	554
555	444	556	655	654	555	655	556	465
666	666	566	456	645	666	544	665	654
454	546	456	546	666	546	545	554	446
464	654	654	564	464	456	466	456	556
3039	3510	3132	3319	3440	3123	3499	3331	3320

Use thumb of right hand to index a zero. Use touch operation.

400	500	550	440	444	555	500	600	50
404	600	650	550	454	666	650	546	400
405	400	440	660	504	444	405	640	505
505	450	600	605	406	404	450	555	605
550	540	550	604	660	505	640	440	445
560	640	406	606	445	606	560	660	664
2824	3130	3196	3465	2913	3180	3205	3441	2669

The 1, 2, 3-Keys

Use first finger on 1-, 4-keys — middle finger on 2-, 5-keys — ring finger on 3-, 6-keys. Use touch operation with machine in proper position.

123	321	456	654	401	410	601	106	152	251	211
411	114	123	321	402	420	602	206	263	362	203
422	225	141	411	403	430	603	306	340	304	356
423	336	252	522	501	150	610	621	114	411	264
101	101	363	633	502	250	620	521	153	351	215
102	201	101	414	503	350	630	421	166	616	106
1582	1298	1436	2955	2712	2010	3666	2181	1188	2295	1355

The 7, 8, 9-Keys

Use first finger on 1-, 4-, 7-keys — middle finger on 2-, 5-, 8-keys — ring finger on 3-, 6-, 9-keys. Go slowly. Develop fluency in tapping the keys.

477	774	707	770	877	778	809	908	159	951	701
588	885	808	880	988	889	887	788	268	862	802
699	996	909	990	577	775	655	556	357	753	903
444	741	478	784	588	858	818	188	488	844	544
474	474	778	854	699	969	718	817	591	195	678
484	444	488	884	998	899	728	827	468	684	809
3166	4314	4168	5162	4727	5168	4615	4084	2331	4289	4437

PRACTICE YOUR TOUCH OPERATION

Instructions: Work each problem twice. Your goal is to match the books' answer. If you do match, go to the next problem—if not, do again.

Set Decimal Selector at 0

(1)	(2)	(3)	(4)	(5)	(6)	(7)	(8)	(9)	(10)
555	665	644	665	465	464	444	665	446	666
444	555	455	446	645	545	555	545	556	555
666	444	566	564	654	546	666	465	655	444
445	666	654	446	456	465	445	556	466	456
554	456	465	556	546	656	546	445	546	546
445	546	645	645	645	646	644	654	654	645
554	645	565	456	654	654	566	465	456	564
454	564	665	464	564	655	454	565	664	564
545	465	546	565	465	566	465	454	465	465
454	456	654	456	456	466	446	546	546	456
545	555	456	564	546	546	665	654	564	645
5661	**6017**	**6315**	**5827**	**6096**	**6209**	**5896**	**6014**	**6018**	**6006**

(11)	(12)	(13)	(14)	(15)	(16)	(17)	(18)	(19)	(20)
456	656	658	459	856	547	586	455	799	133
564	655	548	568	957	478	658	456	989	323
464	545	457	685	745	589	648	454	988	322
565	564	685	485	475	678	458	456	878	212
566	465	548	594	568	456	586	654	897	231
644	546	685	867	587	597	478	466	798	132
564	645	578	749	456	675	448	440	879	213
564	566	586	594	568	475	865	554	978	312
645	556	485	685	579	784	586	564	997	331
684	455	574	856	457	895	486	544	899	233
655	645	856	864	754	786	584	564	889	223
								788	122
6371	**6298**	**6660**	**7406**	**7002**	**6960**	**6383**	**5607**	**10,799**	**2787**

(21)	(22)	(23)	(24)	(25)	(26)	(27)	(28)	(29)	(30)
787	252	288	363	98701	28962	27140	147219	10001	1000
797	282	858	393	10768	316822	34950	85364	40004	4000
878	525	855	636	1236	4687	8792	10652	70007	7000
879	528	525	639	892	27681	14082	2500	20002	2000
898	585	582	696	45316	218021	900	4119	50005	4000
989	858	285	969	381	38719	1645	17270	70006	8000
979	828	528	939	1689	2813	20993	300059	40007	3000
987	852	825	963	20183	105	8777	20611	45000	20008
877	522	882	633	318092	28242	62009	6150	90006	9000
977	822	588	933	25137	3754	14600	30987	87000	3000
788	255	558	366	533	819538	145	8290	56000	30008
798	285	255	396	8021	2891	1005	30005	90007	5000
				5384	99	257	1806	600087	87000
10,634	**6594**	**7029**	**7926**	**536,333**	**1,492,334**	**195,295**	**665,032**	**1,268,132**	**183,016**

ADDITION TRAINING

Instructions: Work each problem once. Your goal is to match the books' answer. If you do match, go to the next problem—if not, work the problem again.

(1)	(2)	(3)	(4)	(5)	(6)	(7)	(8)	(9)	(10)
123	478	147	520	100	753	101	456	546	258
123	102	147	233	200	849	202	456	546	258
456	660	258	700	300	201	303	789	879	369
456	953	258	179	400	694	404	789	879	369
789	879	369	555	500	245	505	321	213	741
789	312	369	310	600	308	606	321	213	741
123	455	147	147	700	617	707	654	546	852
123	878	147	983	800	518	808	654	546	852
456	100	258	258	900	269	909	987	213	963
456	999	258	624	110	703	901	987	213	963
789	644	369	980	120	149	801	321	897	741
789	321	369	161	130	842	701	321	897	741
123	766	147	840	140	303	601	654	564	852
123	330	147	279	150	257	501	654	564	852
5718	7877	3390	6769	5150	6708	8050	8364	7716	9552

(11)	(12)	(13)	(14)	(15)	(16)	(17)	(18)	(19)	(20)
528	160	202	401	987	546	963	369	300	400
639	170	302	301	987	546	963	369	310	304
639	180	402	201	321	879	741	147	230	204
417	190	502	101	321	879	741	147	320	104
417	200	602	100	654	213	852	258	340	903
528	210	702	200	654	213	852	258	350	803
528	220	802	300	987	548	963	369	360	703
417	230	902	400	987	546	963	369	370	603
417	240	102	500	321	879	159	951	380	503
693	250	200	600	321	879	159	951	390	403
693	260	901	700	654	123	357	753	400	303
582	270	801	800	654	123	357	753	410	203
582	280	701	900	987	789	149	941	420	102
369	290	601	107	987	789	149	941	430	300
7449	3150	7722	5611	9822	7952	8368	7576	5010	5838

(21)	(22)	(23)	(24)	(25)	(26)	(27)	(28)	(29)	(30)
208	401	104	124	314	987	974	323	120	256
309	610	106	335	792	776	216	135	551	149
109	102	201	546	689	565	328	545	772	380
307	320	203	757	577	354	431	387	830	277
208	503	305	968	465	143	543	765	941	155
109	530	305	279	353	832	655	554	652	583
307	704	407	413	241	621	767	932	665	352
208	940	409	624	246	497	879	721	478	411
309	305	503	814	148	275	752	722	385	322
107	550	505	225	252	353	533	944	253	685
208	706	606	415	154	511	115	566	141	257
609	660	708	626	266	722	227	788	232	210
407	807	702	816	168	944	499	377	586	556
306	270	900	227	272	177	771	555	752	456
3711	7408	5964	7169	4937	7757	7690	8314	7358	5049

ADDITION TRAINING (*continued*)

(31)	(32)	(33)	(34)	(35)	(36)	(37)	(38)	(39)	(40)
784	225	903	347	903	734	604	233	406	323
656	568	710	258	324	825	831	645	567	564
526	223	507	285	808	528	407	657	816	813
419	114	621	967	216	796	342	186	725	407
308	235	808	788	705	788	209	275	493	324
727	358	432	941	107	194	555	943	338	209
515	102	390	320	309	203	710	338	107	555
201	155	230	930	302	903	833	170	555	701
853	772	149	234	491	701	349	555	902	833
532	803	887	880	878	507	572	902	423	394
411	914	769	126	697	612	681	243	704	527
322	625	582	705	825	880	756	704	318	618
865	566	852	170	528	423	546	138	465	765
527	487	743	309	437	309	332	406	323	604
7646	6147	8583	7260	7530	8403	7727	6395	7142	7637

(41)	(42)	(43)	(44)	(45)	(46)	(47)	(48)	(49)	(50)
705	183	354	755	598	675	209	891	402	189
870	709	465	647	645	764	610	134	353	413
632	111	647	536	924	653	830	905	675	509
544	233	273	689	581	968	425	123	254	321
407	752	158	442	732	244	567	807	308	708
423	468	492	233	476	322	335	690	106	906
509	236	564	958	654	345	240	738	902	875
632	905	859	465	543	456	837	420	378	209
864	324	332	294	323	674	960	533	609	601
257	704	244	851	442	237	708	765	807	803
332	445	986	372	869	185	321	524	123	452
111	236	635	746	356	429	509	380	905	576
907	708	746	654	467	546	431	160	314	353
381	507	557	453	576	895	198	902	981	204
7574	6521	7312	8095	8186	7393	7180	7972	7117	7119

(51)	(52)	(53)	(54)	(55)	(56)
411	375	654	537	289	933
525	283	858	328	335	747
722	371	776	137	147	450
950	532	509	253	565	360
677	443	227	344	482	177
885	523	255	352	393	604
465	984	894	498	631	905
489	564	253	525	509	136
325	588	443	722	406	933
344	767	352	905	771	284
235	590	731	677	630	655
173	272	823	885	540	741
382	255	735	456	477	533
573	114	352	525	339	982
7156	6661	7862	7144	6514	8440

SPEED AND ACCURACY DEVELOPMENT

PROCEDURE FOR SPEED DEVELOPMENT AND PRACTICE

1. Complete each of the Speed Development problems by touch operation, beginning at your accuracy speed until you have obtained the correct answer.

2. Repeat the same problem at a higher and higher speed until an incorrect answer is obtained—then:

3. Slow down your operating speed and repeat that same problem until the correct answer is once again obtained.

4. Move to the next problem and repeat procedures 1, 2, and 3.

PROCEDURE FOR ACCURACY DEVELOPMENT AND PRACTICE

1. Complete each of the Accuracy Development problems and record the answer.

2. To insure correct answers, work at your control speed level. Do not attempt to increase your speed level when accuracy is the primary objective.

PERFORMANCE EVALUATION OF ASSESSMENT PROBLEMS

1. Problem length—expressed in Strokes.

    A. ONE STROKE is counted for each *Key Depression*.
    B. TWO STROKES are counted for each *Plus Key Depression*.

2. Operator speed expressed in Strokes per Minute.

    A. **Gross Strokes per Minute (GS/M)** is computed by multiplying the *TOTAL lines entered per minute × number of strokes per line.*

    Example: You entered a total of 60 lines during a 1-minute, 3-digit test. Compute GS/M as follows:

    Strokes per line:
    3 digits   = 3 strokes
    1 plus key depression   = 2 strokes
                                                   5 strokes per line

    Gross Strokes per line:
         60 (total lines entered)
    ×   5 (strokes per line)
    300 (GS/M)

    B. **Net Strokes per Minute (NS/M)** is computed by multiplying the *CORRECT lines entered per minute × number of strokes per line.*

    Example: If in the example above, you had 3 errors*, you would compute NS/M as follows:

         60 (total lines entered)
    −   3 (lines with errors)
         57 (correct lines entered)
    ×   5 (strokes per line)
    285 (NS/M)

    * An incorrect or omitted digit in any number makes an error of the entire number. Neither the correct digits in the number nor the plus key depression may be counted.

PROCEDURES FOR ASSESSMENT PROBLEMS

1. The purpose of each assessment problem is to determine how many lines you can enter into the machine in ONE MINUTE.

2. When your instructor assigns an Assessment Problem, begin where you see START HERE and complete the column of figures.

3. When you have completed the column, return immediately to the starting point and continue through the column until "time" is called.

4. After the assessment, tear off the machine tape, place the tape alongside the examination problem, check the accuracy of each line and compute GS/M and NS/M (see Performance Evaluation).

5. Record your scores on the machine tape. (Your instructor may select your best score.)

STANDARD OF PERFORMANCE

In order to assist you in determining how your examination results compare with other students who have been tested in the past, the following table has been drawn. [Remember this is only a guide, you may be able to achieve much more.]

End Of	One Minute Exam	Operator Classification NS/M		
		Average	Above Average	Superior
5 hours*	2–3 digits	100–175	176–250	251+
10 hours	3–4 digits	120–195	196–270	271+
	8 digits	100–175	176–250	251+
15 hours	3–4 digits	140–210	211–285	286+
	8 digits	100–175	176–250	251+
20 hours	3–4 digits	150–225	226–300	301+
	8 digits	125–200	201–275	276+

*Based on actual time spent on skill development drills.

Speed Development

ONE-DIGIT PROBLEMS

(1)	(2)	(3)	(4)	(5)	(6)
4	4	3	3	7	4
4	5	3	2	2	7
7	7	5	2	3	5
5	4	3	5	7	3
4	7	2	3	2	2
4	5	3	5	4	7
7	4	2	2	4	5
7	4	5	2	5	3
7	7	3	3	2	5
5	7	2	2	3	4
7	5	2	2	4	3
7	7	3	3	5	2
4	7	2	5	3	5
4	7	2	2	5	4
5	4	5	3	7	4
7	4	3	2	2	2
4	5	5	3	3	7
7	7	2	5	5	3
5	4	2	3	7	2
4	4	3	3	4	7
108	108	60	60	84	84

(7)	(8)	(9)	(10)	(11)	(12)
1	6	8	8	9	3
9	1	0	0	1	3
1	9	6	6	0	1
9	1	0	8	6	6
9	9	6	0	8	8
6	9	8	8	0	4
1	1	0	0	9	7
1	6	0	0	8	0
9	1	6	8	1	2
6	9	8	8	9	9
9	6	8	8	6	5
1	9	8	6	8	0
6	1	0	0	1	4
1	1	0	0	0	2
9	6	8	8	6	7
9	9	0	6	8	6
1	9	8	0	9	8
9	1	6	6	0	9
1	9	0	0	6	1
6	1	8	8	1	5
104	104	88	88	96	90

ONE-DIGIT PROBLEMS

Accuracy Development
ONE-DIGIT PROBLEMS

(1)	(2)	(3)	(4)	(5)	(6)	(7)	(8)
7	4	3	2	5	9	8	1
3	1	4	6	5	4	2	7
4	8	7	9	6	2	1	3
5	9	5	0	7	7	7	4
4	6	8	8	8	6	9	1
7	0	4	0	9	6	1	6
5	8	2	8	1	9	8	8
3	7	7	9	2	7	1	5
5	2	6	9	3	4	6	7
4	5	2	8	4	5	2	2
7	6	9	2	7	5	1	6
3	4	0	6	1	6	2	9
5	1	7	9	5	1	7	5
5	9	4	2	8	2	9	4
7	3	3	8	3	7	1	3
5	2	8	0	6	0	6	2
7	7	2	6	9	8	6	3
3	9	4	0	3	9	2	7
5	3	1	2	7	2	7	8
4	5	5	6	8	3	8	9

Assessment Problems (3 Stroke Units per line)

(9)	(10)	(11)	(12)	A. Start Here	B. Start Here
7	2	6	7	7	7
6	6	8	4	6	8
8	4	0	2	9	3
9	5	4	4	8	0
5	8	1	5	1	2
1	5	2	3	7	8
4	7	3	6	2	9
5	0	5	8	0	4
6	6	4	7	9	3
4	9	6	9	5	6
7	7	9	6	3	1
1	1	8	3	6	9
5	0	7	4	3	0
8	9	4	5	4	4
2	3	1	6	8	5
6	2	5	4	2	7
9	1	2	7	0	1
3	8	8	1	4	5
7	4	3	5	1	2
8	3	4	8	5	6

Return to Starting Point   Return to Starting Point

Note: Turn to Operator Information page 16 and compute GS/M and NS/M.

Speed Development
TWO-DIGIT PROBLEMS

(1)	(2)	(3)	(4)	(5)	(6)
44	87	81	33	10	96
12	46	54	20	17	21
89	13	23	30	33	82
65	65	97	87	90	78
90	13	66	52	14	93
85	97	16	41	86	60
77	32	80	40	34	74
20	30	97	97	69	25
65	98	45	12	84	75
40	21	65	89	50	52
21	40	89	65	52	50
98	65	12	45	75	84
30	20	97	97	25	69
32	77	40	80	74	34
97	85	33	16	60	86
13	90	20	66	96	14
65	65	30	97	21	90
87	89	87	23	82	33
46	12	52	54	78	17
13	44	41	81	93	10
1089	1089	1125	1125	1143	1143

(7)	(8)	(9)	(10)	(11)	(12)
18	93	16	63	50	54
71	12	81	83	73	81
38	78	90	29	45	91
50	93	74	54	38	39
64	40	18	72	66	60
94	66	46	50	27	72
75	65	92	38	82	18
20	32	50	72	40	17
19	28	19	50	93	29
54	70	63	74	60	54
70	54	74	63	54	60
28	19	50	19	29	93
32	20	72	50	17	40
65	75	38	92	18	82
93	94	63	46	54	27
12	64	83	18	81	66
78	50	29	74	91	38
93	38	54	90	39	45
40	71	72	81	60	73
66	18	50	16	72	50
1080	1080	1134	1134	1089	1089

Accuracy Development
TWO-DIGIT PROBLEMS

(1)	(2)	(3)	(4)	(5)	(6)	(7)	(8)
55	35	47	40	63	81	35	93
89	78	53	79	73	45	28	86
80	31	96	86	19	67	44	30
43	58	34	91	70	40	19	39
72	52	25	50	89	10	70	28
59	54	80	56	52	20	38	60
62	84	81	27	30	94	56	17
87	50	17	70	77	33	29	67
60	75	25	38	68	88	54	96
31	24	84	80	42	47	19	63
10	26	69	93	12	85	76	60
97	25	58	14	82	44	51	73
83	78	14	32	59	31	28	40
42	64	94	86	63	87	30	83
40	49	15	52	57	98	69	84
23	32	20	71	17	24	82	50
14	65	80	69	50	22	46	25
66	84	63	13	13	45	70	39
95	53	57	42	37	34	37	38
17	37	86	45	30	15	10	54

(9)	(10)	(11)	(12)	Assessment Problems (4 Stroke Units per line)	
				A. Start Here	B. Start Here
29	27	74	28	76	80
36	39	63	57	96	34
10	40	40	90	25	70
20	82	83	48	10	26
73	40	86	97	76	74
28	17	29	82	94	10
92	50	43	91	80	15
80	82	63	43	43	59
10	52	82	16	15	42
29	93	91	21	69	36
17	87	35	32	85	25
15	72	71	42	20	61
17	19	45	88	34	30
39	38	38	14	20	85
72	45	60	59	76	94
67	89	39	48	35	76
72	17	25	43	14	86
61	60	17	62	90	14
73	38	67	21	84	20
27	91	43	77	57	59
				Return to Starting Point	Return to Starting Point

Speed Development
THREE-DIGIT PROBLEMS

(1)	(2)	(3)	(4)	(5)
999	879	980	179	257
644	312	161	555	695
321	455	840	436	801
766	878	279	674	675
330	100	128	396	169
554	953	310	574	348
201	660	147	869	702
788	102	983	700	851
657	478	258	233	269
221	349	624	520	703
349	221	520	624	149
478	657	233	258	842
102	788	700	983	303
660	201	179	147	753
953	554	555	310	849
879	330	436	128	201
312	766	674	279	694
455	321	396	840	524
878	644	574	161	308
100	999	869	980	761
10 647	10 647	9846	9846	10 854

(6)	(7)	(8)	(9)	(10)
799	456	173	604	340
406	108	205	283	591
437	581	829	506	306
121	256	950	429	829
957	808	719	376	727
728	914	634	685	653
654	756	371	406	480
643	200	283	182	425
309	183	919	574	635
233	927	405	718	927
927	233	718	405	581
183	309	604	919	464
200	643	283	283	390
456	654	506	371	481
108	728	429	634	170
581	957	376	719	528
256	121	685	950	936
808	437	406	829	719
914	406	182	205	208
756	799	574	173	671
10 476	10 476	10 251	10 251	11 061

THREE-DIGIT PROBLEMS

Accuracy Development
THREE-DIGIT PROBLEMS

(1)	(2)	(3)	(4)	(5)	(6)
963	423	691	898	500	918
681	296	762	907	465	824
100	243	384	131	591	606
953	517	605	743	495	371
714	554	185	527	273	693
226	671	369	206	600	417
895	235	445	148	428	684
347	847	207	202	635	738
786	687	745	932	172	539
748	743	815	518	504	405
532	598	239	547	935	271
176	622	200	702	837	536
455	417	841	544	486	824
100	359	602	963	714	606
715	186	725	581	396	372
342	369	347	506	173	594
692	100	131	483	660	195
324	456	709	267	428	564
890	681	898	196	819	505

Assessment Problems (5 Stroke Units per line)

(7)	(8)	A. Start Here	B. Start Here
838	506	526	348
404	928	903	760
685	427	475	951
291	391	358	248
519	273	906	763
371	604	426	902
426	719	911	576
180	592	408	931
373	827	702	807
720	819	343	951
918	270	257	526
728	377	690	361
295	108	952	740
917	624	143	840
406	173	867	341
372	915	188	279
193	192	903	852
724	586	147	534
829	440	625	289
605	883	178	601
		Return to Starting Point	Return to Starting Point

Speed Development

FOUR-DIGIT PROBLEMS

(1)	(2)	(3)	(4)	(5)	(6)
7 887	6 665	1 486	2 030	1 036	7 635
3 300	1 200	2 484	1 683	7 230	2 984
4 566	4 444	5 632	4 529	9 525	3 286
3 200	1 211	1 987	7 426	1 476	1 095
8 779	7 898	3 286	5 600	8 410	1 485
2 133	8 999	3 311	2 000	7 596	9 684
6 455	3 221	7 577	8 954	8 430	2 376
8 900	1 100	9 531	1 596	5 258	2 095
1 223	6 544	9 900	7 847	4 147	3 384
4 500	7 789	1 325	8 746	1 096	9 125
7 789	4 500	8 746	1 325	9 125	1 096
6 544	1 223	7 847	9 900	3 384	4 147
1 100	8 900	1 596	9 531	2 095	5 258
3 221	6 455	2 030	7 577	7 635	8 430
8 999	2 133	1 683	3 311	2 984	7 596
6 665	8 779	4 529	3 286	3 286	8 410
1 200	3 200	7 426	1 987	1 095	1 476
4 444	4 566	5 600	5 632	1 485	9 525
1 211	3 300	2 000	2 484	9 684	7 230
7 898	7 887	8 954	1 486	2 376	1 036
100 014	100 014	96 930	96 930	97 353	97 353

(7)	(8)	(9)	(10)	(11)	(12)
5 826	1 739	5 743	4 182	9 372	2 735
1 222	5 430	6 755	6 294	6 060	9 495
2 596	5 466	5 918	4 050	7 185	2 727
9 383	1 071	4 050	8 191	9 383	6 960
4 861	7 420	9 393	6 040	4 060	9 284
7 633	8 998	4 466	7 186	1 728	3 738
5 281	9 944	9 276	2 927	7 176	8 276
5 555	1 047	8 281	1 836	8 173	4 050
4 736	1 320	5 915	2 738	6 060	3 938
4 728	5 369	5 814	1 739	2 917	9 375
5 369	4 728	1 739	5 814	2 735	2 917
1 320	4 736	4 182	5 915	9 495	6 060
1 739	5 555	6 294	8 281	2 727	8 173
5 430	5 281	4 050	9 276	6 960	7 176
5 466	7 633	8 191	4 466	9 284	1 728
1 071	4 861	6 040	9 393	3 738	4 060
7 420	9 383	7 186	4 050	8 276	9 383
8 998	2 596	2 927	5 918	4 050	7 185
9 944	1 222	1 836	6 755	3 938	6 060
1 047	5 826	2 738	5 743	9 375	9 372
99 625	99 625	110 794	110 794	122 692	122 692

Accuracy Development
FOUR-DIGIT PROBLEMS

(1)	(2)	(3)	(4)	(5)	(6)
3 100	9 733	9 340	7 542	7 652	3 487
8 624	9 052	4 158	5 817	1 490	6 539
3 267	6 644	5 294	6 072	3 853	4 000
9 810	8 711	1 720	5 034	1 425	9 115
5 544	8 923	8 157	4 729	7 001	7 472
7 951	1 597	4 340	9 610	2 862	8 285
3 298	4 545	3 926	2 587	1 516	9 630
1 178	8 901	9 358	1 766	7 360	7 481
4 466	7 623	6 842	6 983	8 534	1 649
2 590	4 286	8 380	3 591	9 937	8 942
3 379	1 300	1 953	8 038	4 892	9 337
5 466	6 465	4 257	2 486	4 169	5 384
8 625	5 286	7 185	8 539	8 347	3 670
3 100	3 010	2 760	6 293	3 659	5 116
9 844	4 849	4 350	4 430	2 000	8 622
2 279	9 722	9 274	1 587	8 915	7 100
3 156	6 513	1 960	7 210	7 742	4 215
7 700	7 070	8 257	2 954	8 625	8 533
9 534	4 359	6 671	1 548	3 960	4 910
8 651	1 568	8 396	3 490	8 741	6 572

Assessment Problems (6 Stroke Units per line)

(7)	(8)	A. Start Here	B. Start Here
7 250	1 783	3 584	2 196
7 285	5 826	9 624	9 320
1 960	2 570	3 376	1 785
1 779	8 125	1 615	9 620
4 350	8 149	8 920	4 763
3 926	8 317	7 020	1 415
9 340	8 430	9 470	8 322
3 729	6 040	3 180	7 680
7 196	2 893	8 634	9 516
6 760	1 641	2 596	4 358
8 173	7 660	7 415	9 076
2 586	1 967	9 154	4 253
7 250	7 239	1 076	8 094
2 815	3 490	2 328	7 781
4 819	9 236	3 695	6 751
1 837	3 540	7 100	5 206
3 840	7 719	8 254	9 344
4 060	9 610	2 674	8 080
9 283	2 875	8 915	3 574
4 161	2 570	3 789	1 239
		Return to Starting Point	Return to Starting Point

Speed Development
FIVE-DIGIT PROBLEMS

(1)	(2)	(3)	(4)	(5)
132 45	220 55	303 32	985 44	869 41
788 66	787 45	767 47	980 15	302 57
979 65	215 44	125 76	323 66	952 06
131 00	649 90	500 00	859 62	330 19
232 56	330 00	875 24	547 88	825 61
131 23	121 32	148 69	632 11	721 09
445 64	667 70	349 78	289 56	867 53
887 99	989 77	378 99	695 24	204 75
125 66	449 85	147 53	119 13	741 58
788 98	300 13	200 00	124 76	178 50
300 13	788 98	124 76	200 00	963 42
449 85	125 66	985 44	147 53	900 19
220 55	887 99	980 15	378 99	635 74
787 45	445 64	323 66	349 78	228 51
215 44	131 23	859 62	148 69	106 74
649 90	232 56	547 88	875 24	398 52
330 00	131 00	632 11	500 00	636 94
121 32	979 65	289 56	125 76	237 48
667 70	788 66	695 24	767 47	104 76
989 77	132 45	119 13	303 32	384 89
9 375 93	9 375 93	9 354 33	9 354 33	10 590 48

(6)	(7)	(8)	(9)	(10)
294 10	969 58	405 07	934 85	405 16
884 32	768 89	155 86	718 69	405 16
241 46	173 93	717 17	148 63	209 18
917 30	456 66	606 54	728 14	383 93
235 76	200 15	233 31	465 30	524 82
841 02	475 82	486 04	939 28	570 00
837 64	594 16	938 34	175 02	719 36
221 33	800 00	696 25	527 39	581 74
917 59	173 52	900 00	291 72	293 72
969 58	457 70	934 85	281 94	664 00
768 89	859 63	718 69	582 76	283 96
173 93	917 59	148 63	900 00	717 39
456 66	221 33	728 14	696 25	482 96
200 15	837 64	465 30	938 34	371 85
475 82	841 02	939 28	486 04	417 65
594 16	235 76	175 02	233 31	928 29
800 00	917 30	527 39	606 54	654 05
173 52	241 46	291 72	717 17	406 05
457 70	884 32	281 94	155 86	175 64
859 63	294 10	582 76	405 07	382 71
11 320 56	11 320 56	10 932 30	10 932 30	9 577 62

FIVE-DIGIT PROBLEMS

Accuracy Development
FIVE-DIGIT PROBLEMS

(1)	(2)	(3)	(4)	(5)	(6)
885 21	495 68	586 84	168 02	415 72	488 08
974 25	112 33	934 25	575 18	923 96	596 32
765 00	206 75	835 73	746 03	378 89	171 40
143 69	436 28	142 60	951 59	142 60	908 02
778 45	705 02	918 53	673 40	867 52	635 73
330 34	586 34	692 47	199 55	163 49	951 24
762 47	634 79	839 50	436 08	701 75	368 41
115 86	138 12	391 60	872 72	776 34	425 72
521 00	909 08	425 01	471 60	809 25	908 31
968 47	292 91	372 46	297 46	436 00	516 95
865 94	748 69	281 60	908 38	596 15	604 03
332 11	102 05	815 75	201 17	808 84	529 08
576 02	685 11	367 40	642 73	236 95	437 76
826 34	742 67	919 55	105 24	411 70	577 01
257 00	433 03	804 36	169 03	289 00	943 61
436 85	548 77	282 77	358 90	375 36	257 68
974 36	963 41	147 60	742 96	421 59	264 01
218 31	506 07	924 76	851 39	148 63	988 73
899 00	524 79	938 09	264 01	275 24	693 29
199 22	125 88	711 02	375 38	138 09	275 14

Assessment Problems (7 Stroke Units per line)

(7)	(8)	A. Start Here	B. Start Here
183 81	183 91	378 90	892 58
404 95	606 91	821 02	347 61
937 60	357 01	353 77	712 49
183 75	937 28	624 75	661 74
405 92	736 95	912 47	853 68
282 73	182 84	343 08	905 02
406 06	672 94	118 61	359 02
583 76	504 06	298 06	417 80
729 14	391 86	596 24	369 43
505 24	275 24	809 41	228 60
193 81	425 05	860 70	435 75
196 06	419 27	353 59	781 19
173 50	673 85	147 63	963 48
827 39	606 04	852 49	289 60
596 37	372 82	714 50	751 47
482 81	295 04	961 40	352 60
492 76	573 81	337 42	151 47
604 05	760 93	586 95	809 53
681 93	594 04	202 87	422 90
425 72	183 81	516 96	167 03
		Return to Starting Point	Return to Starting Point

Speed Development
SIX-DIGIT PROBLEMS

(1)	(2)	(3)	(4)	(5)	(6)
845 312	445 688	208 020	126 899	928 172	184 917
424 701	963 247	635 740	474 258	620 045	381 728
320 078	586 285	200 914	918 296	453 099	691 738
165 320	200 000	675 247	145 989	625 819	718 635
453 365	159 344	348 642	996 303	571 829	728 172
986 204	787 631	358 630	315 705	382 917	391 842
745 322	639 987	963 696	281 740	221 044	814 635
565 500	547 898	982 789	605 050	335 679	172 839
969 950	103 424	298 225	476 301	171 938	939 393
136 687	767 522	389 166	247 369	692 843	271 840
107 899	115 645	416 127	171 938	405 060	718 376
148 604	965 281	475 301	550 700	381 934	827 193
444 478	320 045	963 475	468 921	400 075	291 724
105 685	745 367	802 596	285 286	671 834	506 371
321 265	986 404	178 100	423 000	476 285	183 927
976 120	359 410	258 410	667 755	718 296	292 405
656 600	975 220	695 840	936 815	340 506	819 385
330 155	873 306	584 167	221 345	581 735	376 193
854 369	201 694	941 503	743 762	675 962	281 934
187 099	178 992	773 795	304 743	763 841	147 526
9 744 713	10 922 390	11 150 383	9 362 175	10 418 913	9 740 773

Accuracy Development

Assessment Problems (8 Stroke Units per line)

(7)	(8)	(9)	(10)	A. Start Here	B. Start Here
944 600	148 534	905 174	829 185	238 570	178 534
751 580	399 615	485 260	193 940	911 469	917 899
896 531	183 476	929 150	853 495	853 420	475 268
742 394	896 200	347 634	272 456	177 863	532 903
887 626	258 000	584 059	927 183	963 420	253 680
778 099	371 369	186 142	185 018	752 486	426 801
992 190	912 860	832 199	930 000	511 812	141 684
335 867	785 278	273 506	276 050	873 506	912 596
422 852	932 996	416 847	839 140	992 944	773 490
417 853	173 456	286 359	645 196	358 610	253 788
457 615	112 748	677 671	272 834	931 277	963 217
841 694	369 584	158 436	718 173	368 425	814 690
290 000	738 504	296 148	527 937	963 014	752 674
343 675	217 601	739 240	527 937	752 470	338 041
228 075	848 124	675 360	493 718	189 635	596 257
876 510	695 247	417 250	665 147	942 586	751 486
319 625	285 340	670 913	665 147	743 025	591 000
346 831	334 761	285 250	917 282	891 170	237 510
706 349	907 524	847 506	605 063	639 000	963 420
311 122	576 200	193 380	472 836	742 586	806 342
				Return to Starting Point	Return to Starting Point

Speed Development
SEVEN-DIGIT PROBLEMS

(1)	(2)	(3)	(4)	(5)	(6)
3 368 850	3 365 699	8 680 534	1 234 777	4 081 963	9 372 919
2 379 900	6 752 684	1 021 690	3 812 000	4 081 739	7 296 050
6 479 651	1 962 574	3 486 709	5 739 510	6 518 374	5 837 386
4 789 123	9 334 670	4 352 675	2 520 233	9 283 718	4 042 958
2 223 330	7 596 184	9 086 241	4 961 804	4 472 724	1 783 710
8 746 199	3 224 122	1 982 388	2 347 670	5 040 618	6 062 504
1 676 145	6 763 470	7 739 812	5 852 476	3 728 190	9 171 739
2 258 633	7 789 551	2 476 526	2 851 693	6 359 620	6 372 940
7 898 897	7 112 339	3 399 017	9 904 581	9 518 295	1 934 718
2 345 600	1 549 830	5 863 574	9 510 674	8 517 283	9 382 815
9 415 866	2 081 476	2 885 260	6 250 410	5 406 941	3 728 293
7 763 247	3 000 000	7 185 500	2 566 999	1 719 283	4 604 715
8 900 000	9 635 841	9 416 943	1 752 638	4 527 250	5 169 183
1 211 145	8 825 917	7 914 703	5 840 614	4 752 640	8 373 814
6 944 000	8 765 210	2 614 809	4 724 960	6 841 269	5 406 730
3 575 415	5 842 016	3 435 016	6 677 785	5 183 729	5 828 260
8 765 113	4 176 258	2 796 230	3 395 063	9 514 700	1 919 372
9 544 222	8 452 084	2 415 869	7 283 400	4 367 584	4 728 524
9 675 584	3 438 503	7 410 257	6 960 584	6 618 392	1 583 919
1 278 893	2 199 799	7 594 351	8 153 600	3 950 636	4 272 586
109 239 813	111 868 227	101 758 104	102 341 471	114 484 948	106 873 135

Accuracy Development

Assessment Problems (9 Stroke Units per line)

(7)	(8)	(9)	(10)	A. Start Here	B. Start Here
8 145 700	3 277 450	9 273 596	5 583 924	3 190 367	7 630 913
1 685 234	3 448 090	1 806 539	6 372 861	5 218 916	1 096 472
9 935 476	9 281 566	2 727 741	9 282 716	8 024 572	2 581 097
5 803 369	7 249 530	9 845 416	4 050 606	1 239 516	3 907 804
8 824 700	1 136 788	8 293 675	9 391 738	4 087 093	5 094 867
6 348 596	5 417 267	1 482 000	4 406 850	7 684 950	8 635 749
1 195 141	9 792 200	9 348 530	4 191 835	5 672 401	6 198 125
6 227 626	3 729 633	1 516 890	5 650 650	3 896 152	5 730 201
1 892 377	3 568 415	9 372 576	6 071 927	9 873 424	8 531 692
9 132 040	1 182 689	2 314 480	5 058 249	6 095 871	6 859 164
8 766 521	7 486 302	2 485 369	1 738 272	9 475 368	2 516 983
3 200 000	5 534 740	7 192 582	5 340 606	1 020 357	7 036 709
5 587 897	1 936 948	6 058 446	4 917 381	4 619 586	1 785 906
4 643 211	2 114 590	1 736 731	5 938 605	2 841 243	1 042 765
9 899 544	8 257 695	9 054 300	2 839 172	7 901 852	2 483 456
3 657 952	4 762 680	2 817 360	4 727 140	9 976 307	4 243 789
7 564 231	3 368 090	2 951 674	8 639 172	6 543 842	3 421 482
1 977 841	1 715 247	9 580 147	7 283 914	8 334 075	6 159 321
6 248 700	3 925 900	2 836 752	4 939 456	2 961 358	2 754 208
3 353 289	8 614 158	1 349 068	2 738 140	2 746 901	5 704 338
				Return to Starting Point	Return to Starting Point

Speed Development
EIGHT-DIGIT PROBLEMS

(1)	(2)	(3)	(4)	(5)	(6)
23 456 488	18 625 147	32 398 925	95 396 040	50 404 267	45 729 380
15 763 201	23 578 799	77 156 038	58 504 751	47 528 396	91 763 810
12 233 300	15 742 678	16 751 475	76 254 819	47 600 063	18 172 918
75 258 660	36 783 506	79 287 606	29 140 000	91 739 260	50 681 729
21 324 599	23 596 988	99 254 814	44 115 966	53 928 273	29 341 504
78 751 311	17 483 357	71 760 000	29 258 604	19 600 000	69 381 724
12 576 344	41 425 900	14 763 596	43 476 241	72 860 504	48 172 928
94 369 477	12 123 312	33 384 341	49 526 624	81 717 283	73 837 271
88 989 721	15 760 624	23 842 899	59 614 769	76 050 484	91 346 718
17 889 999	84 946 669	11 228 105	56 414 506	38 173 605	29 257 270
56 314 789	75 369 410	15 963 485	43 526 124	27 392 825	42 576 183
91 557 494	24 000 000	12 892 378	17 604 738	91 738 293	17 192 829
20 547 863	81 763 342	19 100 000	58 124 050	44 038 286	58 172 936
24 876 341	85 985 100	34 763 594	45 804 195	68 172 930	93 852 710
70 000 000	24 852 667	48 526 942	53 455 516	49 283 739	39 385 020
33 124 665	47 946 210	81 966 443	47 635 050	64 027 628	51 728 173
98 975 221	99 999 987	76 425 720	50 691 426	58 173 860	91 583 728
89 006 522	35 863 385	35 852 696	63 495 635	93 982 817	93 817 392
36 968 034	12 114 587	76 157 020	66 546 605	50 017 639	93 827 396
66 754 150	23 753 400	88 347 095	40 675 368	18 195 438	49 173 819
1 028 738 179	801 715 068	949 823 172	1 029 261 027	1 144 625 590	1 178 995 438

Accuracy Development

Assessment Problems (10 Stroke Units per line)

(7)	(8)	(9)	(10)	A. Start Here	B. Start Here
59 633 100	81 121 108	18 176 405	47 382 924	53 416 849	39 855 176
24 256 952	79 622 492	93 929 183	69 191 506	63 802 147	98 919 858
87 641 159	35 967 414	60 524 750	81 735 916	76 032 518	60 027 626
34 325 149	96 352 485	47 283 934	38 171 928	19 200 000	76 713 490
77 543 610	15 969 530	51 674 050	24 845 062	36 742 535	43 522 907
88 435 951	17 736 809	62 938 145	92 938 275	98 186 625	63 488 150
22 678 600	59 938 617	58 682 960	72 860 514	45 714 905	97 104 070
35 344 779	81 742 248	28 371 934	53 739 140	36 959 235	22 274 962
22 678 216	62 719 465	67 292 750	66 725 915	77 714 863	85 359 601
99 870 000	47 383 544	34 040 673	82 817 393	98 143 696	98 538 014
13 386 345	73 928 000	69 181 060	58 274 183	96 328 574	42 586 941
78 991 126	82 718 576	61 729 394	92 763 930	71 357 826	96 378 514
22 578 625	54 320 000	83 742 591	56 640 000	14 090 159	71 423 352
99 000 000	78 886 500	59 371 350	19 283 717	63 048 235	93 248 514
44 358 614	13 669 952	62 685 914	52 486 060	42 109 719	37 100 000
33 167 877	24 655 100	37 182 924	81 729 385	86 682 785	86 257 416
59 841 186	79 741 033	48 174 860	65 543 444	34 091 250	33 347 529
23 244 877	42 688 621	52 928 140	27 163 500	27 643 970	51 486 207
11 496 852	97 441 520	37 182 850	44 567 690	24 762 190	86 349 615
99 087 536	33 579 363	66 573 750	91 743 800	84 321 758	12 936 877
				Return to Starting Point	Return to Starting Point

Speed Development
VARIED-DIGIT PROBLEMS WITH DECIMALS

(1)	(2)	(3)	(4)	(5)	(6)
1.59	16.95	173.83	51,600.00	3,827.16	4,858.68
25.80	15.00	40.60	271.68	93,863.91	917,385.74
.49	748.20	1,938.60	5,242.51	653,225.50	6.86
6.78	3.47	55.04	88,562.10	1,475.36	22,315.00
.99	22.48	8,651.47	330.00	131,477.63	2,416.74
4.11	169.52	27.50	61,959.63	83,728.40	99.25
78.65	7.75	574.24	2,232.22	4,827.50	6.94
.20	984.00	1,934.90	173.96	83,476.82	.33
33.21	3.31	25.86	33,567.78	6,752.90	1,134.00
.89	269.78	122.39	474.81	8,192.99	5,817.43
4.76	91.36	172.96	5,841.43	25,743.47	.92
.57	1.85	173.69	91,899.98	9,183.91	125,522.00
14.86	724.70	4,828.28	17,426.05	495,817.50	6.00
.33	3.93	71.85	448.63	60,638.40	75,862.47
1.20	28.60	3,605.04	5,596.00	525,286.10	7,839.90
96.20	634.85	83.76	9,358.49	6,634.75	19.50
35.00	69.36	7,504.19	917.39	951,447.63	56,918.38
7.54	558.41	934.06	8,372.94	220,000.00	343.67
.24	1.70	57.26	65,147.60	524,147.69	77.42
78.63	2.49	9,183.92	274.77	99,811.98	6.91
392.04	4,357.71	40,159.44	449,697.97	3,989,559.60	1,220,638.14

Accuracy Development

(7)	(8)	(9)
.41	842.67	4,400.21
15.36	9,159.02	48,183.40
9.22	78.34	282,728.39
8.57	251.16	59,195.06
.94	3,762.40	5,706.27
3.36	935.90	39,436.85
8.95	77.10	19,383.91
.21	835.86	2,415.74
.70	281.47	729,381.75
45.76	29.63	4,918.26
2.85	5,367.00	435,691.77
30.10	486.14	28,271.96
.99	5,903.58	8,391.71
8.22	726.81	371,827.00
31.66	99.40	40,667.00
78.00	7,357.10	38,393.75
97.31	226.94	4,405.55
.86	3,585.30	625,042.60
4.50	41.86	566,405.66
4.47	21.49	21,883.99

Assessment Problems

A. Start Here	Stroke Units	B. Start Here	Stroke Units
58.63	6	1.78	5
4.75	11	942,586.30	15
129,602.50	21	.41	19
.40	25	7.69	24
147.68	32	255,920.36	34
.90	36	4.70	39
31,983.01	45	.85	43
2.27	50	33.86	49
34.85	56	1,476.10	59
.76	60	.90	61
962,174.90	70	.25	65
8.83	75	7,421.80	73
5,762.51	83	.34	77
9.43	88	.95	81
.15	92	23,763.89	90
.96	96	1.58	95
8,641.70	104	901.42	102
.43	108	67.53	108
9.82	113	2.41	113
237.50	120	768.09	120

Return to Starting Point / Return to Starting Point

ADDITION AND SUBTRACTION

ADDITION OF NUMBERS WITH DECIMALS

1. When adding numbers containing decimals, enter each number exactly as you would write it. Use the [·], DECIMAL POINT KEY to correctly position the decimal point in each number that you enter.

Example:

8.24
.96
23.19
___
32.39

NOTE!

The decimal selector should be set to accommodate the **largest** decimal addend in each problem.

Solving the Example

STEP 1: Set the Decimal @ 2		
Enter	**Depress**	**Notes**
	[*]	Clears machine
8.24	[+]	
.96	[+]	
23.19	[+]	
	[*]	Total 32.39

PRACTICE PROBLEMS

(1)	(2)	(3)	(4)	(5)	(6)	(7)	(8)
3,545.893	5,984.34	5,906.34	54.94	4.020	.073	.0740294	20.4
8.28	385.25	1.58	1,285.37	91.855	696.6	.0884	558.19
.04	.99	496.20	5,845.29	200.9	1.316	.043	9.002
8.91	5.03	5.55	963.56	.732	49.42	.0000612	237.
237.49	2,934.12	1,583.97	233.33	28.2	9.66	.09027	2.82
8,485.12	506.94	1,275.33	.96	395.270	63.821	.000335	72.593

(9)	(10)	(11)	(12)	(13)	(14)	(15)	(16)
919.46	965.34	64.33	7,593.10	0.4	.020	.0775577	902.
5,196.30	.81	1,978.91	845.38	22.0	.2	.0000004	2.
.76	3,069.11	.04	.76	863.14	3.08	.003227	80.3
35.91	.86	485.19	2,385.18	8.338	.816	.00324	816.
44.23	3,045.76	476.38	5,946.28	9.8	4.744	.0000596	44.74
5,943.22	2.91	.65	.65	7.347	858.535	.00831	535.858
384.11	44.10	4.57	4,578.91	642.785	1.377	.0977	773.1
.95	7.03	3,495.16	.66	80.4	.36	.004	6.3
2,938.93	433.96	458.39	3,496.17	490.45	.066	.017119	660.
185.34	.94	.05	963.86	.8	9.4	.0000008	4.9
6,791.64	1.41	4.49	3,853.11	.54	505.883	.09	883.909
.03	51.24	482.98	1,111.43	97.5	9.	.01969	.9

MIXED DECIMALS

(1)	(2)	(3)	(4)	(5)	(6)	(7)	(8)
98.567	3.57	.005	4.7	136.58	42.376	35.01	253.6
5.32	57.004	7.87	24.98	.983	5.9	.984	5.779
467.96	365.11	74.5	6.752	76.8	579.01	732.9	26.108
.093	57.772	246.897	365.8	6.872	92.475	4.108	.94
25.87	253.9	6.5	.016	769.4	8.97	36.81	8.6
57.9	7.882	38.88	58.9	58.91	.784	4.895	44.81
8.574	46.9	486.119	253.87	6.832	465.8	375.9	776.011
748.107	.753	8.198	58.462	36.1	48.619	8.85	9.35
482.	57.008	.017	721.9	5.19	7.84	.6	.697
57.19	2.1	76.9	76.557	247.881	35.8	363.198	463.9

(9)	(10)	(11)	(12)	(13)	(14)	(15)	(16)
25.896	4.796	253.9	36.982	192.09	89.2	253.68	43.985
.6	25.78	56.895	.87	25.801	.986	.003	45.3
364.89	.842	4.75	432.7	8.9	236.	3.3	4.576
5.551	222.9	365.796	.9	23.08	7.46	22.34	.358
36.8	3.891	57.9	6.89	7.885	.008	.6	45.7
.763	47.9	6.87	.243	323.98	3.87	3.45	.447
8.07	8.35	47.1	34.88	4.874	.764	456.89	387.019
.7	24.9	226.857	.748	36.7	77.011	6.8	56.8
666.19	8.742	30.806	8.92	.345	5.505	4.784	46.1
9.007	182.9	7.73	232.11	6.6	.91	.7	4.964

(17)	(18)	(19)	(20)	(21)
64.975	24.8	65.888	253.8	275.99
354.55	.354	.011	3.456	3.457
3.535	333.7	2.345	3.456	33.1
.56	.506	.4	245.1	3.557
111.	34.6	35.4	3.576	.701
1.1	.99	257.5	55.8	88.109
66.8	86.01	689.	7.876	8.601
76.5	.004	7.9	57.9	8.8
2.674	7.5	24.567	79.63	22.742
.85	464.8	4.08	5.784	56.9

ADDITION WITH ADD MODE

In commercial applications, a majority of the addition problems encountered will involve numbers containing dollars and cents. As an aid to solving these problems, most electronic calculators have a feature called ADD MODE.

ADD MODE assumes that all numbers entered contain 2 digits to the right of the decimal point and will print the number accordingly.

Therefore, the ADD MODE eliminates the entry of the decimal points in numbers containing dollars and cents.

Example:

$$
\begin{array}{r}
\$\ 48.35 \\
32.75 \\
19.00 \\
71.64 \\
\hline
\$171.74
\end{array}
$$

NOTE! When entering a whole number, remember to include the "00" for "no cents," otherwise the machine will misplace the decimal point.

Solving the Example

STEP 1: Set the Decimal @ Add Mode		
Enter	**Depress**	**Notes**
4835	+	Clear machine
3275	+	
1900	+	
7164	+	
	*	Total 171.74

PRACTICE PROBLEMS

(1)	(2)	(3)	(4)	(5)	(6)	(7)	(8)
78.04	2,551.45	48.35	3,864.18	6,496.29	6,496.27	5.93	48.28
4,571.11	6,945.00	3,586.28	2,854.93	5,395.16	4,853.22	5,934.11	6,447.10
687.95	.21	5,693.08	.76	.96	1.56	8.43	678.94
20.10	1.86	.54	32.75	274.29	39.75	800.00	3.35
9.21	386.10	1,111.99	6,845.19	28.45	468.33	3,332.15	2,845.10
3,012.34	5,973.92	.45	.05	2,967.00	.99	667.10	7.00
.56	5,497.57	3,852.19	3,968.49				
777.56	.95	.96	6,597.27				
86.75	2.91	.84	471.64				
91.91	556.78	9,968.27	385.27				
.04	3.78	853.19	395.81				
9,580.32	19.47	44.45	2,384.18				
9,094.34	435.07	3,847.26	5,839.54				
5.41	9,580.73	.65	19.78				
4.98	22.71	903.28	583.54				
47.84	2.26	.99	1,857.39				
574.33	.03	8,589.32	576.64				

CORRECTING ERRORS AND SUBTOTALING

Example:

456.25	
362.93	
411.25	
1230.43	Subtotal
92.18	
255.60	
1578.21	Subtotal
46.30	
985.25	
2609.76	Total

Solving the Example

STEP 1: Set the Decimal @ Add Mode		
Enter	**Depress**	**Notes**
	[*]	Clear machine
456.25	[+]	
362.93	[+]	
411.25	[+]	
	[◊]	Subtotal 1230.43
92.18	[+]	
255.60	[+]	
	[◊]	Subtotal 1578.21
46.30	[+]	
985.25	[+]	
	[*]	Total 2609.76

PRACTICE PROBLEMS

(1)		(2)	
7.02		623.79	
9.10		832.78	
2.41		142.99	
18.53	S	1599.56	S
8.34		756.78	
4.23		335.88	
8.54		795.59	
39.64	S	3487.81	S
23.37		721.66	
16.40		147.68	
13.23		595.45	
22.80		637.69	
115.44	T	5590.29	T

CORRECTING ERRORS

Correcting errors made in entering an amount.

Depress the CLEAR ENTRY key (CE) to remove the amounts that have been entered but not yet added. Then enter the correct amount and continue calculating.

Correcting entries already added into the problem.

If you discover an error after depressing the ADD key, cancel that entry by depressing the MINUS key (this subtracts out the error). Then add the correct number.

If you discover an error after depressing the SUBTRACT key, cancel that entry by depressing the PLUS key (this adds back in the amount of the error). Then subtract the correct number.

ADDITION DEVELOPMENT

Correct machine position and proper operator posture are essential to good figurework production. Check your machine and yourself for good position and posture at the beginning of each lesson.

Addition is used to complete the figurework on most business forms. Typical of most business offices is the daily bank deposit where the receipts are added to determine the amount of the bank deposit.

Note: On pages 37 and 38 the illustration gives an example of the front side of a bank deposit ticket. You, however, are responsible for filling in the back side of the deposit ticket only.

A. Total each column for Scot-Rob Productions bank deposit forms.

B. Write your answers clearly at the bottom of each column.

C. 1. Machine date the tape when starting. (Some machines do not have this feature.)

   2. Using the special key (non-add-print key), number each of the problems on the tape.

D. What decimal selector setting would allow the fastest machine operation?

(Illustration)

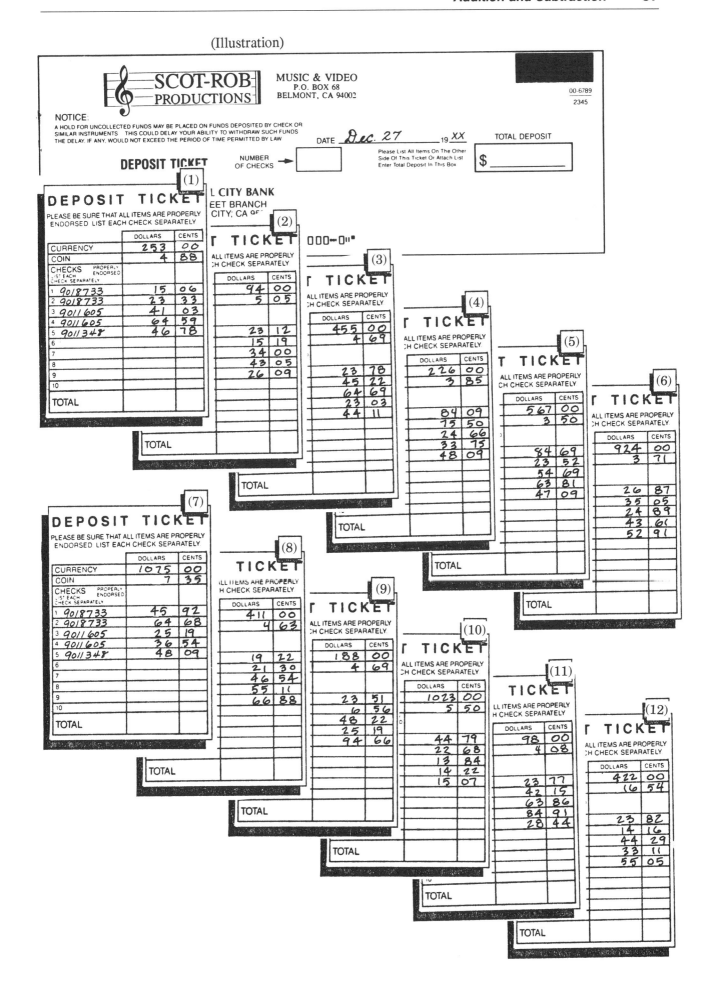

(Illustration)

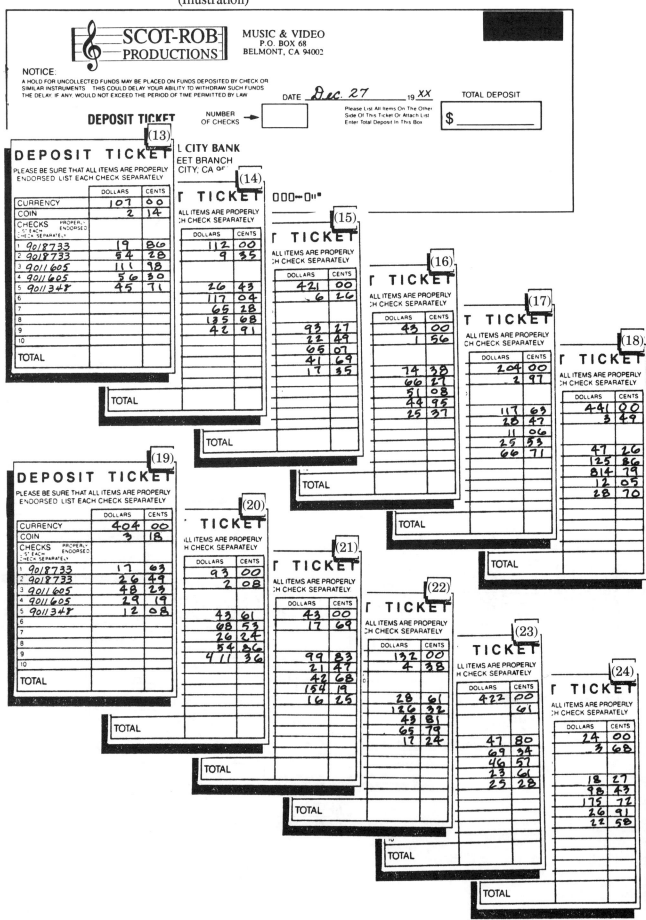

ADDITION AND SUBTRACTION

Solving the Example

Example:
```
  114.23
 − 26.79
    5.24
 ───────
   92.68
```

STEP 1: Set the Decimal @ Add Mode		
Enter	**Depress**	**Notes**
	[*]	Clears calculator
11423	[+]	
2679	[−]	
524	[+]	
	[*]	Total 92.68

PRACTICE PROBLEMS

(1)	(2)	(3)	(4)	(5)	(6)	(7)	(8)
5,943.22	7,213.02	318.46	5,026.29	6.66	75.36	37.18	65.90
−.97	−586.37	−5.27	−54.21	−4.28	−22.94	−21.95	−.85

(9)	(10)	(11)	(12)	(13)	(14)	(15)	(16)
594.96	2.40	9,000.64	1,294.95	86.64	7,937.16	5.19	1.95
−23.96	−1.37	−27.69	−5.93	−1.76	−.89	−.07	−.78

(17)	(18)	(19)	(20)	(21)	(22)	(23)	(24)
6,048.34	648.23	.94	2,592.57	645.37	4.44	5,496.28	945.18
−4,792.01	−486.99	−.27	−16.97	−7.95	−3.18	−3,962.19	−642.57

(25)	(26)	(27)	(28)	(29)	(30)	(31)	(32)
6.95	4,682.91	486.18	21.46	5,083.49	82.91	96.48	2,954.18
−3.46	−17.62	−182.39	−.79	−96.65	−6.66	−31.59	−.06

(33)	(34)	(35)	(36)
.89	5,396.18	.78	6,497.38
2,576.38	6.96 −	8,832.90	18.46 −
846.62 −	284.16	475.91 −	3.98 −
1.11	.57 −	54.72	2,180.11
6,047.22	3,594.19	7.33	453.27

(37)	(38)	(39)	(40)
5,497.18	9.89	5,693.28	.96
79.28	4,857.18	65.38 −	4,364.12
6,396.16 −	56.92 −	4.92	53.29 −
678.38	5,839.15	202.20 −	2.23
2,596.30	5.96	3,851.95	5,361.10
45.98 −	385.92 −	4.59	451.23 −
4.49	9,354.18	3.96	36.12
764.18	6.94 −	5,491.90	1.10
46.81 −	4,592.94 −	45.45 −	3,362.57
4,852.74	18.75	1.29	44.44
12.96	194.86	4,382.19	3,721.87 −
3.95	.07	4.45	50.00

(41)	(42)	(43)	(44)
5.98	5,965.19	54.96	23.10
2,574.19	46.92	3,494.69 −	6,493.90
453.86	.39 −	212.57	57.34
2.91	6,396.19 −	39.60	101.39 −
6,496.93 −	4.58	3,195.80 −	3.47
999.99	683.92	34.56	21.45
5,585.18	34.29 −	2.38	4,574.19
85.29 −	7,485.01 −	6,593.18	371.92 −
.90	9,485.10	54.83	37.18
45.39	8,694.29	364.19 −	175.29 −
9,396.10	991.89	84.29	3.21
1.11 −	5,382.92	4,541.21	3,482.92
38.68	4,378.91	340.17	46.19
.05	548.92	21.33 −	39.27 −
365.96	8,086.45	6,582.19	5,491.73
285.19 −	640.81	1.09	23.10
.67	7.03	454.21	.05 −

CREDIT BALANCE

If a larger number is subtracted from a smaller number, the result will be a negative number. This number is called a CREDIT BALANCE.

When an answer is a CREDIT BALANCE, most machines will print the answer in red.

Solving the Example

Example: 56.23
98.42 –
_____
42.19 –

STEP 1: Set the Decimal @ Add Mode		
Enter	**Depress**	**Notes**
	⊡ *	Clears calculator
5623	⊡ +	
9842	⊡ –	
	⊡ *	Total 42.19 printed in red (negative number or credit balance)

PRACTICE PROBLEMS

(1)	(2)	(3)	(4)
5,984.47	68.95	584.28	226.73 –
8.91	5,844.00	6,714.66 –	2,494.10
6,945.24 –	6,759.12 –	945.92	112.17 –
.09	14.65	.95	33.70
58.26 –	7.95 –	1.11 –	73.58 –
567.26 –	11.93 –	934.72	7,495.20 –

(5)	(6)	(7)	(8)
86.39	55.00 –	5.69	5.97 –
6,496.15 –	5.81	2,484.19 –	48.96
584.23	6,586.92 –	475.92 –	87.55 –
1.91	486.93	78.11	5,495.28
575.97 –	47.81 –	9,694.49 –	7,593.29 –
1,294.04 –	1,756.93 –	.07	19.55
101.33 –	41.95	305.29	22.76 –
5.87	9,495.13 –	6,497.19	14.43 –
93.28 –	58.96	1.59	995.00
12.96	.99	98.10 –	226.65 –
315.37	73.42 –	882.10	894.27
2.05	2.92	4.14	.09

(9)	(10)	(11)	(12)
7.95	1,874.95 –	7,594.91	6,594.28
5,382.18	5,894.11	573.81	65.19 –
748.64 –	93.56	6,597.39 –	4.41
53.76 –	395.20 –	96.30	953.91 –
4,694.72 –	.07	4.44	8,693.03 –
5.82	6,394.19 –	6,592.99 –	11.93
17.55 –	49.12	43.33	.05
2.05	11.92 –	1.18	893.05
64.83 –	85.18	934.19	6,483.09 –
6.32	4.82	931.10	.77 –
893.27 –	202.54 –	32.00	56.23 –
.29	.33	.58	118.64
39.21	39.21 –	101.38	9.33
101.53 –	11.17	1.05 –	11.92 –
3.91	756.12	26.17	23.96
.88 –	845.29 –	22.14	2.92
5,484.17 –	9.46 –	111.17 –	7,968.99

ADDITION AND SUBTRACTION DEVELOPMENT

Add each column of Sales Figures for Scot-Rob Productions and subtract each amount that is circled. Remember to ADD each amount not circled and SUBTRACT each amount if it is circled. Use touch operation. Write answers in TOTAL column.

SCOT-ROB PRODUCTIONS
MUSIC & VIDEO

(1)		(2)		(3)		(4)		(5)		(6)		(7)		(8)		(9)	
Dollars	Cents	Dollars	Cents	Dollars	Cents	Dollars	Cents	Dollars	Cents	Dollars	Cents	Dollars	Cents	Dollars	Cents	Dollars	Cents
8	46	6	01	1	01	18	06	5	06	2	40	7	27	11	02	3	98
7	35	3	25	6	35	4	31	3	19	3	59	6	48	8	93	6	42
3	28	(4	11)		(45)	2	19	2	46	6	77	3	12	9	89	(6	30)
5	48		75	7	89		58	8	15	4	01		88	1	90	4	75
2	69	4	68	6	33	1	47		40	2	58	(4	72)	14	06	7	67
	46	2	01	2	45	3	67		(68)	4	76	16	04	7	76	1	51
(3	78)	3	67		56	8	04	3	47	5	50	(3	48)	8	93		89
4	66	2	89	7	11		56	7	47		41	6	27		42	12	04
2	59		46	3	07	(3	11)	1	15		36	4	56	3	74	1	66
5	11		(21)	4	50	2	50	2	03	(2	45)	9	12	5	25		56
14	66	8	87		68	4	67	4	45	1	19	3	88	11	06	2	60
2	87	6	45	8	24	6	78	6	89	4	22	7	06	(1	63)	3	91
3	49	3	19	5	67	(8	14)	3	01	6	35	1	74	(5	50)	(7	80)
6	25	6	09	8	09	3	50	2	06	(5	12)	5	15	1	49	4	08
5	21	8	11	(4	30)	4	09	4	78	4	08	8	24	5	76	4	61
(3	69)	2	47	9	41	6	84	(8	59)	6	58	1	94	2	24	4	74
4	04	1	80	3	67	2	46	4	12	7	20	(3	86)	4	88	9	85
2	90	2	16	2	43	3	05	1	17	3	59	2	63	8	07	1	42
1	06	(5	05)	4	05	5	15	2	88		66	8	99	1	93	4	73
3	18	7	89	5	68	6	21	4	17	4	12	1	93	(62)		2	55
5	10	4	35	6	30	(3	78)	5	06	6	35	9	09	6	05	10	66
4	60	3	17	2	41	5	42	3	18	7	21	1	48	6	60	3	61
3	87	4	08		47	4	88	6	78		48	6	15	4	29	13	04
Total		Total		Total		Total		Total		Total		Total		Total		Total	

ADDITION AND SUBTRACTION DEVELOPMENT

Add each column of Sales Figures for Scot-Rob Productions and subtract each amount that is circled. Remember to ADD each amount not circled and SUBTRACT each amount if it is circled. Use touch operation. Write answers in TOTAL column.

SCOT-ROB PRODUCTIONS

MUSIC & VIDEO

(10)		(11)		(12)		(13)		(14)		(15)		(16)		(17)		(18)	
Dollars	Cents	Dollars	Cents	Dollars	Cents	Dollars	Cents	Dollars	Cents	Dollars	Cents	Dollars	Cents	Dollars	Cents	Dollars	Cents
5	19	2	67	1	88	7	85	7	33		75		48	1	76	4	14
12	67	8	34	4	71	6	61	6	69	4	61	2	00	8	67	(2	91)
2	04	8	95	5	10	8	01	7	24	7	29	1	20	(1	30)	6	22
(8	80)	6	51	9	35		(72)	4	86	6	42	4	00		49		81
4	10	8	52	(6	74)	1	57	6	74		(63)		32	2	84	3	58
5	54	9	60	4	87	5	06	5	30		79	4	57		98	7	00
8	52	4	35	8	50	7	39	6	49	1	00	(6	42)	6	00	6	47
(3	59)	9	41	5	27		68	(2	65)	3	00	7	59	2	86	2	71
	79	6	08	8	90	1	50		(92)	8	73	(5	28)	6	74		89
1	23	(2	60)		80	8	93	9	82	9	64		(37)	8	16	2	54
1	88	3	99	(1	43)	(1	82)	5	72	3	49		(49)	2	75	(3	66)
7	24		82	5	24		25	8	72	7	31	9	25	1	10		41
14	85	1	39	3	52	2	00		35	(1	65)	7	54		46	8	38
8	34	8	90	1	48	1	45	5	00		47	3	62	(75)		4	69
7	26	1	45	9	70	4	13	1	18		98	7	86	6	13	3	93
1	45	(6	51)	12	35		72	7	23	(1	10)	4	21	9	53		15
1	29	12	01	6	70	(1	75)	4	71	4	54	5	75	(1	89)	6	15
8	38	9	03	4	47		69		36		62	6	73	1	05	2	34
6	70	8	09	5	89	3	75	7	75	6	00	4	00		41	1	60
1	47	1	94	11	02	1	05	4	42		98		80	5	34	1	08
(5	10)	6	41	3	71	1	51	3	29	3	71	4	32	4	56		(85)
8	42	7	64	1	06	7	23	6	96	7	26	4	75	4	27	6	16
9	73	(2	68)	5	35		46		45		47		92		18	4	56
Total		Total		Total		Total		Total		Total		Total		Total		Total	

MULTIPLICATION, DIVISION AND FRACTIONS

MULTIPLICATION

Example: 85.2 × 48 = 4089.6

Solving the Example

STEP 1: Set the Decimal @ 2		
STEP 2: Set Rounding Selector @ 5/4		
Enter	**Depress**	**Notes**
85.2	⊠	Multiplicand
48	⊟	Multiplier
		Total 4089.6 (product)

PRACTICE PROBLEMS

Round all answers to two decimal places.

(1)	(2)	(3)	(4)	(5)	(6)	(7)	(8)	(9)
35.96	49.21	2.111	951.6	.7755	.203	75.91	94.59	31.67
×81	×87	×90	×78	×364	×843	×83	×78	×248

(10)	(11)	(12)	(13)	(14)	(15)	(16)	(17)	(18)
.1491	.6109	38.6	32.10	46.41	267.3	143.2	66.71	99.87
×8	×27	×53	×4	×671	×25	×31	×75	×21

(19)	(20)	(21)	(22)	(23)	(24)	(25)	(26)	(27)
.1616	55.16	1373.864	14.945	754.08	28.83762	310.943	3276.54	750.1869
×88	×72	×.05458	×.4	×92.7	×.76	×32.65	×26.91	×.45

(28)	(29)	(30)	(31)	(32)	(33)	(34)	(35)	(36)
824.58	1936.84	5056.52	279.7584	11.284	759.267	17963.93	.873848	946.832
×.2992	×.2543	×757.4	×.9	×8.32	×5.32	×51.227	×73	×.6

(37)	(38)	(39)	(40)	(41)	(42)	(43)	(44)	(45)
935.586	18.251	21.84	2.485	61.95	959.4	6.953	2.03	76.31
×32	×.429	×.6	×.82	×.87	×4.6	×.27	×.843	×2.48

CHAIN MULTIPLICATION

Solving the Example

Example: $49 \times 3.05 \times .871 = 130.171$

STEP 1: Set the Decimal @ 3		
STEP 2: Set Rounding Selector @ 5/4		
Enter	Depress	Notes
49	$\boxed{\text{x}}$	
3.05	$\boxed{\text{x}}$	
.871	$\boxed{=}$	Total 130.171 (product)

PRACTICE PROBLEMS

Round all answers to 3 decimal places.

(1) $4.91 \times 45 \times 20 =$

(2) $1.86 \times .888 \times 91 =$

(3) $962.5 \times .86 \times 5 =$

(4) $54 \times .77 \times .8 =$

(5) $2.81 \times 94.33 \times 4.71 =$

(6) $683 \times .44 \times 3 =$

(7) $54.5 \times .66 \times 4 =$

(8) $44.10 \times .61 \times 24 =$

(9) $97.8 \times .11 \times 1 =$

(10) $62.03 \times .18 \times 7.01 =$

(11) $76.53 \times 1.29 \times .61 -$

(12) $57.3 \times 52.67 \times 71 =$

(13) $45.76 \times 2.83 \times 30.10 =$

(14) $480.32 \times .15 \times 7 =$

(15) $97.31 \times .86 \times 4.47 =$

(16) $20.93 \times 48.2 \times 78 =$

(17) $726.81 \times 99.43 \times 226.94 =$

(18) $7.24 \times 164 \times 72.96 =$

(19) $28.27 \times 8.39 \times 371.82 =$

(20) $5.98 \times 23.36 \times .94 =$

(21) $726.85 \times 73.75 \times 2.26 =$

(22) $2.267 \times .665 \times 39.74 =$

(23) $75.37 \times 962.24 \times 585.33 =$

(24) $.39 \times 8.22 \times 31.66 =$

(25) $57.18 \times 862.19 \times 193.80 =$

(26) $64.8 \times .32 \times 97 =$

(27) $85.72 \times 5.12 \times .03 =$

(28) $.691 \times 6 \times 14 =$

(29) $16 \times .74 \times 3.2 =$

(30) $1.97 \times 53.09 \times 8.28 =$

(31) $99.2 \times .5 \times 8 =$

(32) $66.55 \times .05 \times 65.11 =$

(33) $99.4 \times .24 \times 39 =$

(34) $65.8 \times 29.3 \times .12 =$

(35) $3.58 \times 5.41 \times 93.8 =$

(36) $60.31 \times 5.05 \times 9 =$

(37) $22.55 \times 66.35 \times 41.21 =$

(38) $58.12 \times 6 \times 4.98 =$

(39) $6.02 \times .01 \times 99 =$

(40) $71.96 \times 22.56 \times 7.18 =$

(41) $281.47 \times 29.63 \times 486.14 =$

(42) $3.94 \times 193.83 \times 24.15 =$

(43) $729.38 \times 4.91 \times 435.69 =$

(44) $41.6 \times 38.39 \times 625.42 =$

(45) $53.67 \times 4.86 \times 5.97 =$

(46) $61.15 \times 42.6 \times 53.9 =$

(47) $41.6 \times 85.39 \times 86.27 =$

(48) $68.14 \times 94.12 \times 766.48 =$

(49) $726.75 \times 58.6 \times 19.38 =$

(50) $555.73 \times 393.52 \times 67.82 =$

CONSTANT MULTIPLICATION

Constant multiplication is when the same number is multiplied by several numbers. In the example, "79" is multiplied by all three numbers. Therefore, "79" is a CONSTANT.

Solving the Example

Example: 79 × 24.21 = 1,912.59
79 × 361.26 = 28,539.54
79 × 204.17 = 16,129.43

STEP 1: Set the Decimal @ 3		
STEP 2: Set Rounding Selector @ 5/4		
Enter	**Depress**	**Notes**
79	⊠ ⊠	
24.21	=	1,912.59 First product
361.26	=	28,539.54 Second product
204.17	=	16,129.43 Third product

PRACTICE PROBLEMS

Remember:
      The CONSTANT is always entered first.

Round all answers to 3 decimal places.

(1) 76.54 x 330.4129 =
(2) 76.54 x 532.690 =
(3) 76.54 x 74.8487 =
(4) 76.54 x 75.6234 =

(5) 85.8942 x 43.889 =
(6) 783.1789 x 43.889 =
(7) 923.7491 x 43.889 =
(8) 8754.752 x 43.889 =

(9) 316.75 x 28.3964 =
(10) 316.75 x 753.872 =
(11) 316.75 x 134.4809 =
(12) 316.75 x .78394 =

(13) .39 x 30.5625 =
(14) .39 x 743.6857 =
(15) .39 x 5824.001 =
(16) .39 x 8.4967 =

(17) 547 x 19.547 =
(18) 547 x 38.4481 =
(19) 547 x 4.8397 =
(20) 547 x 7.54724 =

(21) 62.19 x 295.361 =
(22) 62.19 x 74.8115 =
(23) 62.19 x 425.83 =
(24) 62.19 x 5.4738 =

(25) 9.11 x 47.8791 =
(26) 9.11 x 5.74 =
(27) 9.11 x 643.174 =
(28) 9.11 x .6859 =

(29) 1.4865 x 3.0049 =
(30) 125.678 x 3.0049 =
(31) 9.4705 x 3.0049 =
(32) .07465 x 3.0049 =

(33) 1046.5 x 3.007 =
(34) 1046.5 x .10457 =
(35) 1046.5 x .07453 =
(36) 1046.5 x 6.58114 =

ACCUMULATIVE MULTIPLICATION

Accumulative multiplication is the process of adding the answers of several multiplication problems together to find a grand total.

Solving the Example

Example: $(38 \times 12) + (102 \times 2.4) +$
$(56.1 \times 7.9) = 1,143.99$

STEP 1: Set the Decimal @ 2		
STEP 2: Set Rounding Selector @ 5/4		
Enter	**Depress**	**Notes**
		Clears memory
38	☒ X	
12	☐ = +	456.00 First product
102	☒ X	
2.4	☐ = +	244.80 Second product
56.1	☒ X	
7.9	☐ = +	443.19 Third product
	☐ *	Accumulated products, 1,143.99

PRACTICE PROBLEMS

Round all answers to 2 decimal places.

(1)	(2)	(3)	(4)	(5)	(6)
473 × 172	4.44 × 313	483 × 6.39	.95 × 4.81	777 × 407	.14 × 593
65 × 476	.32 × 864	58 × 7.31	5.38 × 2.48	11 × 663	5.64 × 240
593 × 832	7.54 × 821	943 × 4.91	9.23 × 1.10	256 × 32	1.56 × 181

(7)	(8)	(9)	(10)	(11)	(12)
379 × 5.49	2.71 × 3.74	222 × 5	9.73 × 236	379 × .95	3.38 × 5.57
481 × .358	6.66 × .52	359 × 411	.77 × 3	12 × 1.75	5.16 × .27
573 × .371	2.38 × 3.95	44 × 734	2.80 × 460	809 × 5.49	.988 × 2.05

(13)	(14)	(15)	(16)	(17)	(18)
46 × 644	1.54 × 587	853 × 1.79	5.22 × .05	575 × 833	8.29 × 74
673 × 199	.39 × 25	118 × .38	7.01 × 3.33	72 × 615	.06 × 491
5 × 284	1.11 × 774	378 × 3.97	8.35 × 6.11	988 × 205	.874 × 934

(19)	(20)	(21)	(22)	(23)	(24)
738 × 3.14	6.32 × 3.79	416 × 442	.05 × 225	566 × 4.77	5.86 × 2.83
55 × 4.76	3.00 × .21	664 × 914	3.33 × 7	111 × .84	.147 × 7.82
23 × .41	6.04 × 7.82	829 × 480	1.16 × 538	183 × 4.75	4.75 × 38.4

 Business offices refer to multiplication as "extensions" when multiplying quantity times price on invoices, inventories, and other business forms. An invoice is a bill which itemizes or lists the merchandise shipped to a customer. The invoice also shows the quantity of each item shipped, the price of each item, the total of the bill and the terms of the sale.

• Study the actual invoice forms illustrated on the following pages.

• Extend (multiply) the quantity times the price and enter the answers in extension or total columns of the form.

• Add your extensions and enter total for invoice total.

• Remember to use the accumulator.

INVOICE
NO. *1456*

DATE	*11-12-XX*
SHIP TO	*J. H. MUSIC STORE*
	123 MAIN STREET
	WOODLAND, CA 95695

MUSIC & VIDEO
P.O. BOX 68
BELMONT, CA 94002

SOLD TO: *J. H. MUSIC STORE*
123 MAIN STREET
WOODLAND, CA 95695

ACCOUNT NO.	SALESMAN NO.	PURCHASE ORDER NO.	SHIP VIA	COL	PPD	DATE SHIPPED	TERMS	INVOICE DATE	PAGE
2357	2	N/A	UPS		✓	11-12-XX	Net 30	11-10-XX	1

QTY. ORDERED	QTY. SHIPPED	QTY. BACK ORDERED	ITEM NO.	DESCRIPTION	UNIT PRICE	DISC. %	EXTENDED PRICE	
24	23	1	—	SHEET MUSIC	2.73			(1)
11	11	0	—	SHEET MUSIC - EASY	1.97			(2)
13	13	0	—	PIANO BOOKS	3.49			(3)
17	17	0	—	ORGAN INSTRUCT. BOOK	2.88			(4)
19	19	0	—	BAND METHOD BOOKS	3.17			(5)
146	146	0	—	FINGERING CHARTS	1.56			(6)
98	98	0	—	MANUSCRIPT BOOKS	1.64			(7)
12	12	0	—	FLASH CARD SETS	2.49			(8)
6	6	0	—	FAKE BOOKS	16.57			(9)
17	15	2	—	AUTOHARP METHOD	3.76			(10)
21	21	0	—	GUITAR CHORD BOOK	1.97			(11)
14	14	0	—	VOCAL SELECTION BOOK	5.68			(12)
11	11	0	—	PIANO/ORGAN CHORD BOOK	1.83			(13)
18	18	0	—	KEYBOARD CHARTS	1.92			(14)
37	30	7	—	EASY PIANO BOOKS	2.37			(15)
9	9	0	—	SCHIRMER LIBRARY	6.84			(16)
14	14	0	—	SCHAUN NOTESPELLER	2.91			(17)
21	20	1	—	CLASSICAL PIANO SOLOS	4.29			(18)
					SALE AMOUNT			(19)
					MISC. CHARGES		N/A	
					SALES TAX		35.79	
					FREIGHT			
				THANK YOU	TOTAL			(20)

INVOICE
NO. *1459*

SCOT-ROB PRODUCTIONS
MUSIC & VIDEO
P.O. BOX 68
BELMONT, CA 94002

DATE	*12-9-XX*
SHIP TO	*MUSIC CENTER*
	321 ELM STREET
	WOODLAKE, CA 95000

SOLD TO: *MUSIC CENTER*
321 ELM STREET
WOODLAKE, CA 95000

ACCOUNT NO.	SALESMAN NO.	PURCHASE ORDER NO.	SHIP VIA	COL	PPD	DATE SHIPPED	TERMS	INVOICE DATE	PAGE
A-694	*3*	*509*	*UPS*		*✓*	*12-9-XX*	*1%10-Net 30*	*12-11-XX*	*1*

QTY. ORDERED	QTY. SHIPPED	QTY. BACK ORDERED	ITEM NO.	DESCRIPTION	UNIT PRICE	DISC. %	EXTENDED PRICE	
2	*2*	*0*	*1210 HS*	*SPEAKER ENCLOSURE*	*114.75*			(1)
3	*3*	*0*	*70*	*STR. PHONE PLUG*	*2.13*			(2)
12	*12*	*0*	*PV*	*PEAVEY MICROPHONE*	*30.85*			(3)
10	*10*	*0*	*SS*	*20' PRO CABLE*	*6.38*			(4)
3	*3*	*0*	*8-PAK*	*MICROPHONE WIND SCREEN*	*7.50*			(5)
3	*3*	*0*	*12AX7*	*SUPER 7" VACUUM TUBE*	*5.50*			(6)
7	*7*	*0*	*SA-1*	*PEAVEY STAND ADAPTOR*	*8.00*			(7)
4	*4*	*0*	*5221*	*12" GRILLE KIT*	*3.98*			(8)
2	*2*	*0*	*EDI*	*DIRECTOR BOX*	*24.97*			(9)
3	*3*	*0*	*5299*	*5' Y-STEREO PATCH CABLE*	*8.50*			(10)
2	*2*	*0*	*CT-1*	*PEAVEY CABLE TESTER*	*17.48*			(11)
2	*2*	*0*	*5240*	*72"x36" BLK GRILL CLOTH*	*9.50*			(12)
2	*0*	*2*	*5211*	*BLACK TOUCH UP PAINT*	*2.48*			(13)
3	*3*	*0*	*5180*	*REC. HANDLE ASSEMBLY*	*4.98*			(14)
4	*4*	*0*	*5160*	*AMP RUBBER FEET*	*1.75*			(15)
2	*2*	*0*	*5172*	*FLITE CASE LATCH*	*4.98*			(16)
3	*3*	*0*	*5071*	*REPL. SW REMOTE PEDAL*	*2.00*			(17)
4	*4*	*0*	*5120*	*SWIVEL CASTER*	*2.25*			(18)
6	*6*	*0*	*5080*	*GUITAR STRAP BUTTON*	*1.00*			(19)

SALE AMOUNT		(20)
MISC. CHARGES	*3.00*	
SALES TAX	*N/A*	
FREIGHT	*43.19*	
TOTAL		(21)

THANK YOU

DIVISION

Example: 1,404 ÷ 12 = 117

Solving the Example

STEP 1: Set the Decimal @ 2		
STEP 2: Set Rounding Selector @ 5/4		
Enter	**Depress**	**Notes**
1404	÷	Dividend
12	=	Divisor
		Answer 117.00 (quotient)

PRACTICE PROBLEMS

Round all answers to 4 decimal places.

(1) 2,365,942 ÷ 4,603 =

(2) 9.8654 ÷ .52341 =

(3) 7,731,695 ÷ 3,144 =

(4) 109.54 ÷ 21.08 =

(5) 595,175 ÷ 5,742 =

(6) 4,698,425 ÷ 481.6 =

(7) 3,235,310 ÷ 26,841 =

(8) 1,986,375 ÷ 48,765 =

(9) 5,484,853 ÷ 476 =

(10) 42,598.28 ÷ .5009 =

(11) 348,525 ÷ 5,863 =

(12) 948.526 ÷ 58.29 =

(13) 1,926.00 ÷ 486.542 =

(14) 6.2359 ÷ .0086 =

(15) 9,628 ÷ 451 =

(16) 629.15 ÷ 456.84 =

(17) 13.8 ÷ 63.16 =

(18) 5.9826 ÷ .0068 =

(19) 625,849 ÷ 928.5 =

(20) 51,542 ÷ 59,818.33 =

(21) 820,185 ÷ 4,645 =

(22) 8,131,525 ÷ 6,136 =

(23) 5,383 ÷ 9,761 =

(24) 35,965 ÷ 5,523 =

(25) 711,520 ÷ 44,869 =

(26) 3,994,546 ÷ 7,315 =

(27) 890 ÷ 16 =

(28) 525,843 ÷ 3,685 =

(29) 5,181,125 ÷ 442,789 =

(30) 992,874 ÷ 625 =

(31) 386.78 ÷ 82.15 =

(32) .2564 ÷ .25 =

(33) 245.15 ÷ 818.93 =

(34) .52 ÷ 86.9 =

(35) .25 ÷ 9.68 =

(36) .5246 ÷ .52 =

(37) 6,786.83 ÷ 48.3575 =

(38) 9,876.83 ÷ 1,280 =

(39) 4,591.75 ÷ 1,456.25 =

(40) 526,948 ÷ 98.986 =

CONSTANT DIVISION

Constant division is when several numbers are all divided by the same number. In the example, all three numbers are divided by "44,869." Therefore, "44,869" is a CONSTANT DIVISOR.

Example: 711,520 ÷ 44,869 = 15.86
598,620 ÷ 44,869 = 13.34
461,023 ÷ 44,869 = 10.27

Solving the Example

STEP 1: Set the Decimal @ 2		
STEP 2: Set Rounding Selector @ 5/4		

Enter	Depress	Notes
44869	÷ ÷	
711520	=	Answer 15.86 First quotient
598620	=	Answer 13.34 Second quotient
461023	=	Answer 10.27 Third quotient

PRACTICE PROBLEMS

Round all answers to 2 decimal places.

(1) 22 ÷ 6.034 =
(2) 364.01 ÷ 6.034 =
(3) 642.3 ÷ 6.034 =

(4) 264.98 ÷ 101.503 =
(5) 877.623 ÷ 101.503 =
(6) 1245.93 ÷ 101.503 =

(7) 122.66 ÷ 25.018 =
(8) 68.425 ÷ 25.018 =
(9) 885.001 ÷ 25.018 =

(10) 643.122 ÷ .84517 =
(11) 379.4815 ÷ .84517 =
(12) 57.3771 ÷ .84517 =

(13) 411.03 ÷ 166.574 =
(14) 1052.78 ÷ 166.574 =
(15) 923.56 ÷ 166.574 =

(16) 2544.006 ÷ 1,379.46 =
(17) 3467.1249 ÷ 1,379.46 =
(18) 8360.01 ÷ 1,379.46 =

(19) 9,832 ÷ .10406 =
(20) 1.49756 ÷ .10406 =
(21) 3.2245 ÷ .10406 =

(22) 101.446 ÷ 98.003 =
(23) 1352.29 ÷ 98.003 =
(24) 995.04 ÷ 98.003 =

(25) 844.6133 ÷ 561.8204 =
(26) 562.9205 ÷ 561.8204 =
(27) 1540.831 ÷ 561.8204 =

(28) 55.49 ÷ 2.00409 =
(29) 386.5412 ÷ 2.00409 =
(30) 1,479.2214 ÷ 2.00409 =

(31) 36,472 ÷ 533 =
(32) 61,298 ÷ 533 =
(33) 54,196 ÷ 533 =

(34) 89,216 ÷ 421 =
(35) 25,711 ÷ 421 =
(36) 57,190 ÷ 421 =

(37) 21,560 ÷ 815 =
(38) 61,458 ÷ 815 =
(39) 23,842 ÷ 815 =

(40) 41,950 ÷ 1542 =
(41) 967,846 ÷ 1542 =
(42) 513,189 ÷ 1542 =

(43) 5942 ÷ 415 =
(44) 7224 ÷ 415 =
(45) 1379 ÷ 415 =

(46) 4118 ÷ 502 =
(47) 9526 ÷ 502 =
(48) 8727 ÷ 502 =

(49) 4116 ÷ 619 =
(50) 3267 ÷ 619 =
(51) 1752 ÷ 619 =

(52) 6727 ÷ 732 =
(53) 9362 ÷ 732 =
(54) 6828 ÷ 732 =

DECIMAL EQUIVALENTS OF FRACTIONS

To solve a problem involving fractions on a calculator, it is necessary to determine the DECIMAL EQUIVALENT of the fraction.

These problems are solved by dividing the NUMERATOR by the DENOMINATOR.

Solving the Example

Example: $\dfrac{9}{16} = .5625$

STEP 1: Set the Decimal @ 4		
STEP 2: Set Rounding Selector @ 5/4		
Enter	**Depress**	**Notes**
9	÷	
16	=	Answer 0.5625 (decimal equivalent)

PRACTICE PROBLEMS

Round all answers to 4 decimal places.

(1) $\dfrac{2}{6} =$　　(2) $\dfrac{3}{6} =$　　(3) $\dfrac{4}{6} =$　　(4) $\dfrac{5}{6} =$　　(5) $\dfrac{2}{8} =$

(6) $\dfrac{3}{8} =$　　(7) $\dfrac{4}{8} =$　　(8) $\dfrac{5}{8} =$　　(9) $\dfrac{1}{6} =$　　(10) $\dfrac{6}{12} =$

(11) $\dfrac{1}{4} =$　　(12) $\dfrac{7}{8} =$　　(13) $\dfrac{1}{9} =$　　(14) $\dfrac{2}{9} =$　　(15) $\dfrac{3}{9} =$

(16) $\dfrac{1}{8} =$　　(17) $\dfrac{11}{12} -$　　(18) $\dfrac{3}{5} -$　　(19) $\dfrac{5}{9} -$　　(20) $\dfrac{6}{9} =$

(21) $\dfrac{7}{9} =$　　(22) $\dfrac{8}{9} =$　　(23) $\dfrac{6}{8} =$　　(24) $\dfrac{2}{4} =$　　(25) $\dfrac{1}{2} =$

(26) $\dfrac{2}{12} =$　　(27) $\dfrac{3}{12} =$　　(28) $\dfrac{4}{12} =$　　(29) $\dfrac{5}{12} =$　　(30) $\dfrac{4}{9} =$

(31) $\dfrac{4}{5} =$　　(32) $\dfrac{3}{4} =$　　(33) $\dfrac{7}{12} =$　　(34) $\dfrac{8}{12} =$　　(35) $\dfrac{9}{12} =$

(36) $\dfrac{10}{12} =$　　(37) $\dfrac{1}{12} =$　　(38) $\dfrac{2}{3} =$　　(39) $\dfrac{1}{3} =$　　(40) $\dfrac{35}{12} =$

(41) $\dfrac{47}{196} =$　　(42) $\dfrac{75}{82} =$　　(43) $\dfrac{49}{295} =$　　(44) $\dfrac{1}{5} =$　　(45) $\dfrac{2}{5} =$

ADDITION AND SUBTRACTION OF FRACTIONS

1. For each mixed number to be ADDED:
   a. Find the decimal equivalent of the fractional portion of the mixed number and add it to the Accumulator.*
   b. Enter the whole number portion of the mixed number and add it to the Accumulator.

2. For each mixed number to be SUBTRACTED:
   a. Find the decimal equivalent of the fractional portion of the mixed number and subtract it from the Accumulator.
   b. Enter the whole number portion of the mixed number and subtract it from the Accumulator.

3. When all of the mixed numbers have been added to (subtracted from) the Accumulator, press the TOTAL KEY

*An internal memory.

Example: $154 \frac{11}{16}$

$- 27 \frac{7}{12}$

$\overline{127.1042}$

Solving the Example

STEP 1: Set the Decimal @ 4

STEP 2: Set Rounding Selector @ 5/4

Enter	Depress	Notes
11	$\div$	
16	$= +$	0.6875 Decimal equivalent of $\frac{11}{16}$
154	$+$	
7	$\div$	
12	$= -$	0.5833 Decimal equivalent of $\frac{7}{12}$
27	$-$	
	$*$	Answer 127.1042

PRACTICE PROBLEMS

Round all answers to 4 decimal places.

(1)	(2)	(3)	(4)	(5)
$117 \frac{7}{16}$	$7 \frac{3}{8}$	$362 \frac{1}{6}$	$43 \frac{1}{8}$	$103 \frac{3}{4}$
$- 32 \frac{1}{16}$	$- 5 \frac{1}{3}$	$- 75 \frac{1}{8}$	$- 5 \frac{1}{4}$	$- 15 \frac{3}{8}$

(6)	(7)	(8)	(9)	(10)
$119 \frac{1}{4}$	$101 \frac{2}{3}$	$85 \frac{3}{16}$	$567 \frac{11}{16}$	$67 \frac{5}{12}$
$- 76 \frac{1}{2}$	$- 40 \frac{7}{12}$	$- 80 \frac{3}{8}$	$- 265 \frac{5}{16}$	$- 12 \frac{1}{2}$

(11)	(12)	(13)	(14)	(15)
$158 \frac{3}{8}$	$88 \frac{1}{16}$	$199 \frac{1}{12}$	$25 \frac{1}{2}$	$35 \frac{7}{8}$
$25 \frac{1}{8}$	$140 \frac{7}{8}$	$18 \frac{1}{6}$	$- 265 \frac{5}{16}$	$119 \frac{1}{4}$
$10 \frac{1}{4}$	$9 \frac{2}{3}$	$75 \frac{5}{8}$	$43 \frac{3}{12}$	$98 \frac{3}{8}$
$9 \frac{3}{16}$	$50 \frac{5}{16}$	$85 \frac{3}{16}$	$7 \frac{3}{8}$	$76 \frac{1}{2}$
$101 \frac{2}{3}$	$- 12 \frac{7}{12}$	$145 \frac{7}{8}$	$80 \frac{1}{6}$	$103 \frac{3}{4}$
$40 \frac{7}{12}$	$201 \frac{1}{3}$	$- 2 \frac{1}{4}$	$47 \frac{1}{2}$	$53 \frac{1}{16}$
$- 35 \frac{1}{4}$	$3 \frac{1}{8}$	$80 \frac{3}{8}$	$567 \frac{11}{16}$	$15 \frac{3}{8}$
$- 21 \frac{1}{3}$	$15 \frac{1}{6}$	$67 \frac{5}{12}$	$14 \frac{7}{12}$	$- 7 \frac{2}{3}$

MULTIPLICATION OF MIXED NUMBERS

1. Find the decimal equivalent of the fractional portion of the MULTIPLICAND and add it to the MEMORY.

2. Enter the whole number portion of the MULTIPLICAND and add it to the MEMORY.

3. Find the decimal equivalent of the fractional portion of the MULTIPLIER and add it to the ACCUMULATOR.

4. Enter the whole number portion of the MULTIPLIER and add it to the ACCUMULATOR.

5. Multiply the total of the ACCUMULATOR by the total of the MEMORY.

Example: $154\frac{11}{16}$ multiplicand

$\times 27\frac{7}{12}$ multiplier

$\overline{4266.7917}$

PRACTICE PROBLEMS

Round all answers to 4 decimal places.

(1)	(2)	(3)	(4)
$87\frac{5}{7}$	$453\frac{3}{9}$	$75\frac{4}{16}$	$437\frac{2}{7}$
$\times 23\frac{1}{16}$	$\times 19\frac{1}{2}$	$\times 23\frac{1}{3}$	$\times 221\frac{4}{9}$

(5)	(6)	(7)	(8)
$94\frac{1}{2}$	$281\frac{2}{5}$	$119\frac{1}{5}$	$102\frac{5}{7}$
$\times 7\frac{3}{5}$	$\times 8\frac{3}{16}$	$\times 7\frac{1}{4}$	$\times 14\frac{1}{8}$

(9)	(10)	(11)	(12)
$15\frac{3}{8}$	$103\frac{3}{4}$	$98\frac{3}{8}$	$46\frac{3}{16}$
$\times 7\frac{2}{3}$	$\times 53\frac{1}{6}$	$\times 76\frac{1}{2}$	$\times 2\frac{1}{4}$

Solving the Example

STEP 1: Set the Decimal @ 4		
STEP 2: Set Rounding Selector @ 5/4		
Enter	**Depress**	**Notes**
11	÷	
16	M+	.6875
154	M+	154.0000
7	÷	
12	=+	0.5833
27	+	
	*	27.5833
	X	Multiplier
	M*	Multiplicand from memory
	=	4266.7917 Product

(13)	(14)	(15)	(16)	(17)	(18)	(19)	(20)
$12\frac{1}{12}$	$12\frac{1}{2}$	$362\frac{1}{6}$	$23\frac{3}{4}$	$25\frac{1}{8}$	$40\frac{7}{12}$	$35\frac{1}{4}$	$80\frac{3}{8}$
$\times 5\frac{1}{3}$	$\times 70\frac{3}{16}$	$\times 75\frac{1}{8}$	$\times 5\frac{1}{4}$	$\times 10\frac{1}{4}$	$\times 35\frac{1}{8}$	$\times 21\frac{1}{3}$	$\times 67\frac{5}{12}$

DIVISION OF MIXED NUMBERS
Solving the Problems

1. Find the decimal equivalent of the fractional portion of the DIVISOR and add it to the Memory.

2. Enter the whole number portion of the DIVISOR and add it to the Memory.

3. Find the decimal equivalent of the fractional portion of the DIVIDEND and add the whole number portion to the Accumulator. Divide this total by the Memory Total.

Example: $154\frac{11}{16} \div 27\frac{7}{12} = 5.6080$

PRACTICE PROBLEMS

Round all answers to 4 decimal places.

(1) $7\frac{1}{3} \div 1\frac{1}{3} =$

(2) $4\frac{2}{3} \div 2\frac{1}{3} =$

(3) $\frac{3}{4} \div 1\frac{1}{2} =$

(4) $1\frac{1}{6} \div \frac{7}{8} =$

(5) $\frac{5}{9} \div \frac{5}{8} =$

(6) $8\frac{3}{4} \div 6\frac{2}{3} =$

(7) $\frac{1}{8} \div 1\frac{1}{3} =$

(8) $\frac{3}{4} \div \frac{3}{5} =$

(9) $7\frac{1}{2} \div 1\frac{1}{3} =$

(10) $3\frac{1}{2} \div 2\frac{3}{4} =$

Solving the Example

STEP 1: Set the Decimal @ 4		
STEP 2: Set Rounding Selector @ 5/4		

Enter	Depress	Notes
7	÷	
12	M+	0.5833
27	M+	
11	÷	
16	=+	0.6875
154	+	
	*	154.6875 Dividend
	÷	
	M*	Divisor
	=	Answer = 5.6080

(11) $1\frac{1}{3} \div 3\frac{2}{3} =$

(12) $3\frac{3}{4} \div 2\frac{1}{2} =$

(13) $5\frac{1}{4} \div 3\frac{1}{2} =$

(14) $5\frac{1}{8} \div 3\frac{3}{9} =$

(15) $1\frac{1}{2} \div 2\frac{1}{2} =$

(16) $2\frac{5}{8} \div 1\frac{3}{4} =$

(17) $4\frac{2}{3} \div 9\frac{1}{2} =$

(18) $8\frac{3}{4} \div 6\frac{2}{3} =$

(19) $1\frac{5}{9} \div 3\frac{1}{3} =$

(20) $3\frac{1}{3} \div 2\frac{1}{2} =$

REVIEW OR QUIZ PROBLEMS—MIXED NUMBERS

Round all answers to 4 decimal places.

(1)	(2)	(3)	(4)	(5)
$43\frac{3}{12}$	$35\frac{1}{3}$	$3\frac{1}{8}$	$38\frac{4}{5}$	$4\frac{11}{12}$
$75\frac{5}{8}$	$41\frac{2}{7}$	$35\frac{1}{4}$	$94\frac{2}{3}$	$75\frac{1}{8}$
$9\frac{2}{3}$	$39\frac{2}{5}$	$80\frac{3}{16}$	$48\frac{5}{8}$	$32\frac{1}{5}$
$10\frac{1}{4}$	$91\frac{1}{8}$	$567\frac{1}{2}$	$246\frac{5}{14}$	$76\frac{1}{2}$

(6)	(7)	(8)	(9)	(10)
$42\frac{3}{16}$	$59\frac{5}{12}$	$113\frac{1}{2}$	$81\frac{4}{9}$	$43\frac{1}{8}$
$-23\frac{3}{4}$	$-32\frac{11}{12}$	$-53\frac{1}{16}$	$-27\frac{6}{11}$	$-7\frac{3}{8}$

(11)	(12)	(13)	(14)	(15)
$112\frac{11}{16}$	82	$165\frac{4}{7}$	$19\frac{7}{12}$	$45\frac{6}{7}$
$\times\ 3\frac{1}{8}$	$\times 32\frac{1}{8}$	$\times 50\frac{1}{4}$	$\times\ 69$	$\times 90\frac{1}{2}$

(16) $21\frac{1}{3} \div 15\frac{1}{6} =$

(17) $67\frac{5}{12} \div 14\frac{7}{12} =$

(18) $88\frac{1}{6} \div 25\frac{1}{2} =$

(19) $864\frac{4}{5} \div 29\frac{7}{8} =$

(20) $462\frac{1}{12} \div 51\frac{7}{12} =$

(21) $211\frac{4}{5} \div 28\frac{1}{6} =$

PERCENT

PERCENTAGE

For a more complete explanation of percentage see the *Business Mathematics Review*, page one.

FINDING THE PERCENTAGE

Example: What is 16% of $795?

Formula:

$$\underset{(\$\,Amount)}{Base} \times \underset{(\%\,Sold)}{Rate} = \underset{(\$\,Sold)}{Percentage}$$

Solving the Example

STEP 1: Set the Decimal @ 2		
STEP 2: Set Rounding Selector @ 5/4		
Enter	**Depress**	**Notes**
795	X	Base
16	%	Rate
		Percentage = 127.20

PRACTICE PROBLEMS

Round all answers to 2 decimal places.

(1) What is 81% of $865?

(2) What is 72% of $7894?

(3) What is 37% of $101?

(4) What is 3% of $6541?

(5) What is 98% of $2587?

(6) What is 16% of $106?

(7) What is 69% of $6580?

(8) What is 30% of $547?

(9) What is 17% of $6855?

(10) What is 45% of $892?

(11) What is 48% of $5573?

(12) What is 41% of $2900?

(13) What is 53% of $1588?

NOTE!

In using the % Key the decimal is automatically placed correctly.

(14) What is 93% of $445?

(15) What is 29% of $745?

(16) What is 92% of $1104?

(17) What is 71% of $3876?

(18) What is 6% of $24?

(19) What is 33% of $1212?

(20) What is 97% of $7832?

(21) What is 9% of $451?

(22) What is 61% of $786?

(23) What is 23% of $8439?

(24) What is 33% of $3845?

(25) What is 69% of $574?

(26) What is 31% of $5896?

FINDING THE BASE VALUE

Formula: Base = Percentage ÷ Rate

Example: 493.27 is 51% of what number?

Solving the Example

STEP 1: Set the Decimal @ 2		
STEP 2: Set Rounding Selector @ 5/4		
Enter	**Depress**	**Notes**
493.27	÷	Percentage
51	%	Rate
		Base = 967.20

PRACTICE PROBLEMS

Round all answers to 2 decimal places.

(1) $1633.50 is 65.5% of

(2) $2753.94 is 36.5% of

(3) $421.10 is 37.2% of

(4) $987.42 is 56.3% of

(5) $92.13 is 10.6% of

(6) $3605.44 is 27.9% of

(7) $1159.73 is 23.0% of

(8) $340.19 is 129% of

(9) $772.49 is 117% of

(10) $506.77 is 48.1% of

(11) $1666.11 is 95.6% of

(12) $700.03 is 12.3% of

(13) $769.94 is 45.5% of

(14) $2341.94 is 118% of

(15) $488.77 is 133% of

(16) $606.88 is 45.9% of

(17) $1159.72 is 78.1% of

(18) $1531.76 is 17.7% of

(19) $3840.51 is 19.2% of

(20) $1578.35 is 28.5% of

(21) $1485.57 is 15.5% of

(22) $894.17 is 75.3% of

(23) $991.82 is 91.6% of

(24) $35.98 is 45.1% of

(25) $589.46 is 17.1% of

(26) $465.63 is 22.3% of

(27) $7893.11 is 87.3% of

(28) $662.39 is 67.4% of

(29) $21.76 is 29.3% of

(30) $4583.98 is 121% of

FINDING THE RATE (PERCENT)

1. When comparing the relationship between two numbers, the PERCENT is found by dividing.

2. To find what percent one number is of another, you must:
   a. Determine which number is the 100% portion, and
   b. Determine which number is the one being compared.

3. Use the formula to find your answer.

   Formula: Rate = Percentage ÷ Base

   Example: What percent of 930 is 187?

The number following "of" is usually the 100% number or the base.

Solving the Example

STEP 1: Set the Decimal @ 2		
STEP 2: Set Rounding Selector @ 5/4		
Enter	**Depress**	**Notes**
187	÷	Percentage
930	%	Base
		Rate = 20.11%

PRACTICE PROBLEMS

Round all answers to 2 decimal places.

WHAT % OF:

 (1) $5744.66 is $2934.78
 (2) $7378.73 is $567.77
 (3) $7893.62 is $544.89
 (4) $242.99 is $44.23
 (5) $5500.00 is $1672.87
 (6) $3985.12 is $2834.65
 (7) $745.69 is $345.19
 (8) $7854.10 is $754.93
 (9) $8451.73 is $1833.67
(10) $721.30 is $55.46
(11) $3755.73 is $2834.57
(12) $5969.00 is $4783.17
(13) $743.23 is $22.22
(14) $8348.75 is $465.29
(15) $3743.98 is $1824.99
(16) $475.82 is $5.86
(17) $385.29 is $262.38
(18) $5742.92 is $3741.19
(19) $1240.32 is $5211.56
(20) $8891.55 is $4732.93
(21) $867.00 is $353.17
(22) $5749.29 is $38.77
(23) $4732.92 is $2831.99
(24) $8949.92 is $3333.99
(25) $7894.00 is $4389.11
(26) $5645.01 is $6238.45
(27) $6239.50 is $920.57
(28) $722.56 is $23.44
(29) $4644.30 is $374.96
(30) $3119.39 is $1782.93

WHAT % IS:

 (1) $1809.77 of $5748.39
 (2) $1843.52 of $2745.93
 (3) $75.89 of $6893.72
 (4) $894.82 of $1837.28
 (5) $289.64 of $79.11
 (6) $793.42 of $2845.71
 (7) $1784.63 of $8956.45
 (8) $605.11 of $3845.21
 (9) $1809.40 of $4833.89
(10) $7849.92 of $9343.74
(11) $450.00 of $895.96
(12) $561.33 of $643.19
(13) $1487.53 of $1759.33
(14) $47.28 of $91.22
(15) $8475.17 of $9384.50
(16) $3845.16 of $6743.93
(17) $485.92 of $1832.44
(18) $485.13 of $617.33
(19) $398.10 of $583.20
(20) $5843.93 of $8934.10
(21) $3854.91 of $7940.33
(22) $932.10 of $1564.88
(23) $761.75 of $1839.75
(24) $75.39 of $594.10
(25) $928.34 of $4674.37
(26) $7892.11 of $9457.94
(27) $891.02 of $7843.37
(28) $3841.81 of $4783.46
(29) $1554.27 of $2893.29
(30) $571.94 of $8754.33

REVIEW OR QUIZ PROBLEMS
Percent

Round all answers to 2 decimal places.

(1) What is 18% of 36?

(2) 25% of 52 =

(3) What is $37\frac{1}{2}$% of 40?

(4) What is $\frac{1}{2}$% of 6500?

(5) 1633.50 is 65.5% of ?

(6) 465.63 is 22.3% of ?

(7) 50% of what number is 48?

(8) 25% of what number is 10?

(9) 5% of what amount is $3.00?

(10) $5\frac{1}{4}$% of what amount is 126.00?

WHAT PERCENT OF:

(11) 340 is 15.30?

(12) $67,392.60 is $5,615.05?

(13) 21,690 is 28,920?

(14) 254 is 86?

(15) $500.00 is $14.50?

(16) 4,525 is 56.5% of _____ .

(17) 4,270 is _____ % of 8,329.

(18) 62.2% of 1,985 = _____ .

(19) 1,833 is _____ % of 7,621.

(20) 44.3% of 1,371 = _____ .

(21) 1,065 is 48% of _____ .

(22) 374 is _____ % of 981.

(23) 725 is 17% of _____ .

(24) 61% of 1,938 = _____ .

(25) 752 is _____ % of 3,424.

PERCENT INCREASE AND DECREASE

Many businesses use comparisons of expenses, profits, sales, etc., from one period to another as a means of determining trends which can be used as a basis for future planning, measuring current success or failure, etc.

Formulas:

Amount of Change (increase or decrease)
= Present Years' Amount
− Previous Years' Amount

Percent of Change (increase or decrease)
= Amount of Change
÷ Previous Years' Amount

Example:

Sales (Present Year)	Sales (Previous Year)
$821,457	$490,321
$586,541	$761,870

Amount of Change Increase/Decrease	Percent of Change Increase/Decrease
$331,136	67.53% Increase
−$175,329	23.01% Decrease

Some machines have a symbol, Δ% (meaning Delta percent), which can be used in calculating Increase and Decrease problems as illustrated by the tapes below.

Solving the Example

STEP 1: Set the Decimal @ 4		
STEP 2: Set Rounding Selector @ 5/4		

Enter	Depress	Notes
821457	+	
490321	%	
		331,136.00 Amount of increase 67.53% Increase
586541	+	
761870	%	
		175,329.00 Amount of decrease 23.01% Decrease

Illustration 1

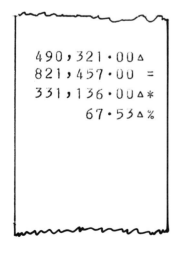

Illustration 2

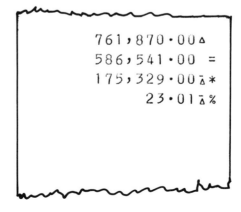

 Always enter the present year first except when using a Delta Percent Key

PRACTICE PROBLEMS

Instructions: In your answers, indicate Increase by INC and Decrease by DEC. Round all answers to 4 decimal places.

 A positive answer indicates an increase. A negative answer, which is printed in red with a minus sign (−), indicates a decrease.

This Year	Last Year	Amount of Increase/Decrease	Percent of Increase/Decrease
$ 1,256.34	$ 961.46	(1) $ _____	(2) _____ %
$ 2,796.61	$ 1,894.55	(3) $ _____	(4) _____ %
$ 3,468.52	$ 2,137.64	(5) $ _____	(6) _____ %
$ 3,861.45	$ 4,612.83	(7) $ _____	(8) _____ %
$ 5,318.62	$ 4,937.51	(9) $ _____	(10) _____ %
$ 7,684.53	$ 6,134.97	(11) $ _____	(12) _____ %
$ 8,761.88	$ 9,875.24	(13) $ _____	(14) _____ %
$10,532.46	$ 11,468.39	(15) $ _____	(16) _____ %
$13,467.92	$ 9,341.57	(17) $ _____	(18) _____ %
$15,682.47	$ 14,235.81	(19) $ _____	(20) _____ %
$16,483.72	$ 12,457.83	(21) $ _____	(22) _____ %
$17,392.48	$ 19,375.64	(23) $ _____	(24) _____ %
$46,132.79	$ 23,457.86	(25) $ _____	(26) _____ %
$68,241.39	$ 93,142.21	(27) $ _____	(28) _____ %
$88,551.43	$101,345.67	(29) $ _____	(30) _____ %

PERCENT DISTRIBUTION

In many businesses, once the total sales, expenses, profits, etc. have been determined, they then calculate what percent of the total has been obtained by each department. The total of the percents must equal 100.*

Formula:

$$\text{Percent of Sales} = \frac{\text{Department Sales}}{\text{Total Sales}}$$

1. Find the TOTAL SALES. To eliminate re-entry of this number, store this total in the Memory.

2. Perform the first division problem...

Dept. A ÷ Total Sales

3. ACCUMULATE your answers in the Memory to check that your total equals 100%.

Example:

Compute the percent of sales for each department.

Dept.	Sales		Percent
A	$425.25	.4692 =	46.92%
B	334.34	.3689 =	36.89%
C	146.68	.1619 =	16.19%
	$906.27		100.00%

Solving the Example

STEP 1: Set the Decimal @ 4		
STEP 2: Set Rounding Selector @ 5/4		
Enter	**Depress**	**Notes**
425.25	[+]	
334.34	[+]	
146.68	[+]	
	[*]	906.27 Total sales
	[M+]	
425.25	[÷]	
	[M*]	
	[= +]	46.92% = Dept. A
334.34	[= +]	36.89% = Dept. B
146.68	[= +]	16.19% = Dept. C
	[*]	Total = 100.00%

* If the TOTAL PERCENT does not equal 100%, add or subtract .01 from the largest one or two numbers.

Example: If the total is 100.02%, subtract .01 from each of the two largest numbers.

If the total is 99.99%, add .01 to the largest amount.

PRACTICE PROBLEMS

Round all answers to 2 decimal places with decimal selector set at 4.

Dept.	Amount		Percent
A	$ 225.00	(2)	
B	335.00	(3)	
C	346.00	(4)	
	(1) $		100%
D	$ 6,789.37	(6)	
E	1,845.48	(7)	
F	930.00	(8)	
G	564.22	(9)	
H	1,485.83	(10)	
	(5) $		100%
I	$11,645.69	(12)	
J	20,834.23	(13)	
K	67.54	(14)	
L	716.92	(15)	
M	1,493.90	(16)	
	(11) $		100%
N	$ 6,894.93	(18)	
O	574.19	(19)	
P	1,743.69	(20)	
Q	381.22	(21)	
	(17) $		100%
R	$21,473.08	(23)	
S	581.10	(24)	
	(22) $		100%
T	$12,455.00	(26)	
U	1,640.00	(27)	
V	2,499.00	(28)	
W	876.00	(29)	
X	5,444.00	(30)	
	(25) $		100%

REVIEW OR QUIZ PROBLEMS
Percent Increase and Decrease and Percent Distribution

Find the amount of change and the percent increase or decrease of the following:

This Year	Last Year	Amount of Increase/Decrease	Percent of Increase/Decrease
(1) $ 1,750.38	$ 1,500.49	a.) $ _____	b.) _____ %
(2) $ 1,650.31	$ 1,425.86	a.) $ _____	b.) _____ %
(3) $425,000.00	$450,000.00	a.) $ _____	b.) _____ %
(4) $ 2,278.54	$ 2,391.62	a.) $ _____	b.) _____ %
(5) $ 8,475.17	$ 9,384.50	a.) $ _____	b.) _____ %

Find the percent distribution of the following:

Dept.	Amount	Percent
A	$ 1,845.48	(7) _____
B	$20,834.23	(8) _____
C	$ 2,574.19	(9) _____
D	$12,473.08	(10) _____
	(6) $ _____	_____ 100%

MARK-UP BASED ON COST

The following terms are used in mark-up calculations:

Cost   —   The purchase price of an item.
Selling Price   —   The amount for which something is sold.
Mark-Up   —   The amount which is added to the cost to obtain the selling price.
% Mark-Up   —   A percent, based on either the cost or selling price, that is used to determine the markup.

Formulas:

Mark-Up   = Cost × % Mark-Up

Selling Price   = Cost + Mark-Up

Example:

Cost	% Mark-Up	Mark-Up	Selling Price
$68.27	45.5%	?	?

Solving the Example

STEP 1: Set the Decimal @ 2		
STEP 2: Set Rounding Selector @ 5/4		
Enter	**Depress**	**Notes**
68.27	[X]	
45.5	[%]	$31.06 Mark-up
	[+]	$99.33 Selling price

PRACTICE PROBLEMS

Round all answers to 2 decimal places.

Cost	% Mark-Up	Mark-Up	Selling Price
$245.00	15.5 %	(1) $ _____	(2) $ _____
$ 51.23	56. %	(3) $ _____	(4) $ _____
$ 67.71	25.5 %	(5) $ _____	(6) $ _____
$ 88.21	31.5 %	(7) $ _____	(8) $ _____
$ 9.78	40.5 %	(9) $ _____	(10) $ _____
$111.67	23.5 %	(11) $ _____	(12) $ _____
$ 38.70	22.5 %	(13) $ _____	(14) $ _____
$ 5.40	30. %	(15) $ _____	(16) $ _____
$218.59	12.5 %	(17) $ _____	(18) $ _____
$ 74.62	28.5 %	(19) $ _____	(20) $ _____
$800.00	33.33%	(21) $ _____	(22) $ _____
$950.29	25. %	(23) $ _____	(24) $ _____
$ 47.26	28.6 %	(25) $ _____	(26) $ _____
$ 55.95	42.5 %	(27) $ _____	(28) $ _____
$295.65	65.5 %	(29) $ _____	(30) $ _____

PERCENT MARK-UP BASED ON COST

Formulas:

Mark-Up = Selling Price − Cost

% Mark-Up = Mark-Up ÷ Cost

Example:

Cost	Selling Price	% Mark-Up	Mark-Up
$18.65	$29.95	?	?

Solving the Example

STEP 1: Set the Decimal @ 2		
STEP 2: Set Rounding Selector @ 5/4		

Enter	Depress	Notes
29.95	[+]	
18.65	[M+]	
	[−]	
	[*]	$11.30 Mark-up
	[÷]	
	[M*]	
	[%]	60.59% Percent of mark-up

PRACTICE PROBLEMS

Round all answers to 2 decimal places.

Cost	Selling Price	Mark-Up	% Mark-Up
$ 4.95	$ 6.49	(1) $ _____	(2) _____ %
$ 10.42	$ 19.98	(3) $ _____	(4) _____ %
$ 21.50	$ 28.39	(5) $ _____	(6) _____ %
$ 71.39	$ 88.50	(7) $ _____	(8) _____ %
$ 61.80	$ 99.25	(9) $ _____	(10) _____ %
$ 104.25	$ 119.49	(11) $ _____	(12) _____ %
$ 233.00	$ 288.59	(13) $ _____	(14) _____ %
$ 546.31	$ 709.95	(15) $ _____	(16) _____ %
$ 882.34	$ 995.00	(17) $ _____	(18) _____ %
$ 726.48	$ 979.33	(19) $ _____	(20) _____ %
$ 1,463.82	$ 1,650.00	(21) $ _____	(22) _____ %
$ 1,050.05	$ 1,339.50	(23) $ _____	(24) _____ %
$ 13,467.54	$ 16,888.25	(25) $ _____	(26) _____ %
$ 38,426.00	$ 48,277.13	(27) $ _____	(28) _____ %
$101,250.00	$120,000.00	(29) $ _____	(30) _____ %

MARK-UP BASED ON SELLING PRICE

Formulas:

$$\text{Selling Price} = \frac{\text{Cost}}{100\% - \%\text{ Mark-Up}}$$

Mark-Up = Selling Price − Cost

1. Find (100% − % Mark-Up) and convert the answer to a decimal.
2. Solve the formulas.

Example:

Cost	% Mark-Up	Mark-Up	Selling Price
$68.27	40%	?	?

100% − 40% = 60% = .60 (complement)

Solving the Example

STEP 1: Set the Decimal @ 2		
STEP 2: Set Rounding Selector @ 5/4		
Enter	**Depress**	**Notes**
68.27	M −	
	÷	
.60	M +	$113.78 Selling price
	M*	$45.51 Mark-up

PRACTICE PROBLEMS

Round all answers to 2 decimal places.

Cost	% Mark-Up	Mark-Up	Selling Price
$ 63.78	32 %	(1) $ _____	(2) $ _____
$ 35.69	43 %	(3) $ _____	(4) $ _____
$105.35	31 %	(5) $ _____	(6) $ _____
$ 44.27	43 %	(7) $ _____	(8) $ _____
$117.47	45.5 %	(9) $ _____	(10) $ _____
$ 58.15	21.5 %	(11) $ _____	(12) $ _____
$226.49	40 %	(13) $ _____	(14) $ _____
$ 71.11	38.5 %	(15) $ _____	(16) $ _____
$413.20	42.5 %	(17) $ _____	(18) $ _____
$ 97.62	28 %	(19) $ _____	(20) $ _____
$ 79.26	52.5 %	(21) $ _____	(22) $ _____
$314.49	25.5 %	(23) $ _____	(24) $ _____
$501.53	13.9 %	(25) $ _____	(26) $ _____
$622.94	34.5 %	(27) $ _____	(28) $ _____
$ 72.44	40 %	(29) $ _____	(30) $ _____

PERCENT MARK-UP BASED ON SELLING PRICE

Formulas:

Mark-Up = Selling Price − Cost

% Mark-Up = $\dfrac{\text{Mark-Up}}{\text{Selling Price}}$

Example:

Cost	Selling Price	% Mark-Up	Mark-Up
$68.25	$98.50	?	?

Solving the Example

STEP 1: Set the Decimal @ 2		
STEP 2: Set Rounding Selector @ 5/4		

Enter	Depress	Notes
98.50	[+] [M+]	
68.25	[−]	
	[*]	
	[÷]	30.25 Mark-up
	[M*]	
	[%]	30.71% Percent mark-up

PRACTICE PROBLEMS

Round all answers to 2 decimal places.

Cost	Selling Price	Mark-Up	% Mark-Up
$ 3.88	$ 5.49	(1) $ _____	(2) _____ %
$ 6.71	$ 7.19	(3) $ _____	(4) _____ %
$ 10.88	$ 12.88	(5) $ _____	(6) _____ %
$ 4.39	$ 4.50	(7) $ _____	(8) _____ %
$ 24.20	$ 29.95	(9) $ _____	(10) _____ %
$ 111.00	$ 119.50	(11) $ _____	(12) _____ %
$ 225.18	$ 298.25	(13) $ _____	(14) _____ %
$ 362.10	$ 399.95	(15) $ _____	(16) _____ %
$ 489.39	$ 501.80	(17) $ _____	(18) _____ %
$ 1,463.87	$ 1,888.00	(19) $ _____	(20) _____ %
$ 1,649.28	$ 1,995.00	(21) $ _____	(22) _____ %
$ 4,000.00	$ 5,134.79	(23) $ _____	(24) _____ %
$10,080.60	$11,249.49	(25) $ _____	(26) _____ %
$15,643.77	$17,777.25	(27) $ _____	(28) _____ %
$26,000.00	$27,034.64	(29) $ _____	(30) _____ %

REVIEW OR QUIZ PROBLEMS
Mark-Up

I. Complete the following **mark-up based on cost** problems:

	Cost	Selling Price	Mark-Up	% Mark-Up
(1)	$21.50	$ _____	$6.89	_____ %
(2)	$ _____	$288.59	$55.59	_____ %
(3)	$726.48	$ _____	$ _____	34.80 %
(4)	$ _____	$48,277.13	$9,851.13	_____ %
(5)	$61.80	$99.25	$ _____	_____ %

II. Complete the following **mark-up based on selling price** problems:

	Cost	Selling Price	Mark-Up	% Mark-Up
(6)	$ _____	$17,777.25	$2,133.48	_____ %
(7)	$1,649.28	$ _____	$345.72	_____ %
(8)	$489.39	$501.80	$ _____	_____ %
(9)	$24.20	$ _____	$ _____	19.20 %
(10)	$1,463.87	$1,888.00	$ _____	_____ %

Formulas: *MARKUP ON COST*

Mark-Up = Cost × % Mark-Up
Selling Price = Cost + Mark-Up
Mark-Up = Selling Price − Cost
% Mark-Up = Mark-Up ÷ Cost

Formulas: *MARKUP ON SELLING PRICE*

$$\text{Selling Price} = \frac{\text{Cost}}{100\% - \% \text{ Mark-Up}}$$

Mark-Up = Selling Price − Cost

$$\% \text{ Mark-Up} = \frac{\text{Mark-Up}}{\text{Selling Price}}$$

INVOICING

Formulas:

Extension	=	Quantity × Price
Sub-Total	=	Sum of the Extensions
Tax	=	Sub-Total × % Tax
Net Amount	=	Sub-Total + Tax

Example:

Description	Quantity	Unit Price	Amount
SF201	8	$ 4.23	$ 33.84
L6009	24	$ 3.00	72.00
AC250	12	$ 16.95	203.40
FI118	18	$ 2.49	44.82
		Sub-Total	$354.06
		5% Tax	17.70
		Net Amount	$371.76

PRACTICE PROBLEMS

Round all answers to 2 decimal places.

Description	Quantity	Unit Price	Extension
X4QTC	120	$ 1.37	$_____(1)
BCT90	64	2.46	$_____(2)
AXZ20	24	4.39	$_____(3)
TC641	3	16.79	$_____(4)
B362S	112	4.82	$_____(5)
QT241	36	.65	$_____(6)
C49QT	85	1.09	$_____(7)
		Sub-Total	$_____(8)
		Sales Tax 6%	$_____(9)
		Total	$_____(10)

QT8D	3	16.86	$_____(1)
C160	8	29.95	$_____(2)
641B	12	79.40	$_____(3)
C362	21	19.55	$_____(4)
C241	6	32.50	$_____(5)
		Sub-Total	$_____(6)
		Sales Tax 6%	$_____(7)
		Total	$_____(8)

Solving the Example

STEP 1: Set the Decimal @ 2

STEP 2: Set Rounding Selector @ 5/4

Enter	Depress	Notes
8	[x]	
4.23	[= +]	
24	[x]	
3	[= +]	
12	[x]	
16.95	[= +]	
18	[x]	
2.49	[= +]	
	[◇]	$354.06 Subtotal
	[x]	
5	[%]	$17.70 Amount of tax
	[+]	$371.76 Net amount

INVOICING PRACTICE PROBLEMS

Customer
Purchases

Video Tapes

Description Stock Numbers	Quantity	Unit Price	Extension
QT8DC	17	$ 6.13	$ _____ (1)
49AF2	9	18.49	$ _____ (2)
CS241	8	49.73	$ _____ (3)
TS428	12	4.98	$ _____ (4)
K4DCB	45	.20	$ _____ (5)
		Sub-Total	$ _____ (6)
		Sales Tax 5%	$ _____ (7)
		Total	$ _____ (8)

Description Stock Numbers	Quantity	Unit Price	Extension
BCD49	63	$ .85	$ _____ (1)
Q49AC	120	1.38	$ _____ (2)
EH600	12	6.43	$ _____ (3)
MNC45	24	12.95	$ _____ (4)
STN30	36	8.50	$ _____ (5)
		Sub-Total	$ _____ (6)
		Sales Tax 6%	$ _____ (7)
		Total	$ _____ (8)

Description Stock Numbers	Quantity	Unit Price	Extension
DC48T	13	$ 2.49	$ _____ (1)
CS362	4	349.50	$ _____ (2)
QTD80	6	21.35	$ _____ (3)
NO431	62	2.49	$ _____ (4)
CXD98	55	3.88	$ _____ (5)
C49QT	12	12.77	$ _____ (6)
		Sub-Total	$ _____ (7)
		Sales Tax 5½%	$ _____ (8)
		Total	$ _____ (9)

Description Stock Numbers	Quantity	Unit Price	Extension
TR490	16	$ 5.73	$ _____ (1)
XYZ30	12	9.64	$ _____ (2)
BCXY2	4	17.68	$ _____ (3)
QT241	24	3.49	$ _____ (4)
HIQ30	9	46.38	$ _____ (5)
4QCST	11	8.16	$ _____ (6)
		Sub-Total	$ _____ (7)
		Sales Tax 6½%	$ _____ (8)
		Total	$ _____ (9)

CASH DISCOUNTS

It is common business practice to offer a buyer the privilege of deducting a certain percent from the amount of the bill for early payment. The amount deducted is known as a CASH DISCOUNT.

Formulas:

Amount of Discount = Amount of Bill
$\qquad$ × % Discount

Net Amount = Amount of Bill
$\qquad$ − Amount of Discount

Example:

Amount of Bill	% Discount	Amount of Discount	Net Amount
$129.83	8%	?	?

 If the machine does not have a Percent Key, you must change the percent to a decimal.

Solving the Example

STEP 1: Set the Decimal @ 2		
STEP 2: Set Rounding Selector @ 5/4		
Enter	**Depress**	**Notes**
129.83	☒ x	
8	☒ %	10.39 Amount of discount
	☐ −	119.44 Net amount
	☐ +	

PRACTICE PROBLEMS

Round all answers to 2 decimal places.

List Price	% Discount	Amount of Discount	Net Amount
$345.67	33½%	(1) _____	(2) _____
$ 53.90	25 %	(3) _____	(4) _____
$375.91	14 %	(5) _____	(6) _____
$110.76	16 %	(7) _____	(8) _____
$ 89.94	40 %	(9) _____	(10) _____
$195.60	27½%	(11) _____	(12) _____
$ 76.18	19 %	(13) _____	(14) _____
$321.75	45 %	(15) _____	(16) _____
$554.69	17½%	(17) _____	(18) _____
$159.48	44 %	(19) _____	(20) _____
$108.93	12 %	(21) _____	(22) _____
$558.67	37 %	(23) _____	(24) _____
$169.73	22 %	(25) _____	(26) _____
$ 86.93	29 %	(27) _____	(28) _____
$531.82	38 %	(29) _____	(30) _____

TRADE DISCOUNTS

In order to adjust list prices published in catalogs, many manufacturers and wholesalers use TRADE DISCOUNTS. A trade discount may involve more than one discount as seen in the example.

Example:

List Price	% Discount	Amount of Discount	Net Amount
$525.00	25-15-5	?	?

The first discount is taken off the list price, the second off the list price less the first discount, etc. The above example would be solved as follows:

$$\begin{array}{rl}
 & \$525.00 & = & \text{list price} \\
25\% \text{ of } \$525.00 = & -131.25 & = & 25\% \text{ discount} \\
\hline
 & \$393.75 & = & \text{1st Net Amt.} \\
15\% \text{ of } \$393.75 = & -59.06 & = & 15\% \text{ discount} \\
\hline
 & \$334.69 & = & \text{2nd Net Amt.} \\
5\% \text{ of } \$334.69 = & -16.73 & = & 5\% \text{ discount} \\
\hline
 & \$317.96 & = & \text{final Net Amt.}
\end{array}$$

NOTE!

Amount of discount = Sum of discounts

or

Amount of discount = List Price
− Net Amount

Solving the Example

STEP 1: Set the Decimal @ 2		
STEP 2: Set Rounding Selector @ 5/4		

Enter	Depress	Notes
525	M+	
	X	
25	%	131.25 First discount
	−	393.75 First net amount
	X	
15	%	59.06 Second discount
	−	334.69 Second net amount
	X	
5	%	16.73 Third discount
	−	
	M−	
	M*	317.96 Final net amount
		207.04 Total discount

PRACTICE PROBLEMS

Round all answers to 2 decimal places.

List Price	Trade Discounts	Amount of Discount	Net Amount
$179.45	20/15/5	(1) _____	(2) _____
$196.45	40/20/5	(3) _____	(4) _____
$225.95	7½/5½/5	(5) _____	(6) _____
$107.00	18/15/5	(7) _____	(8) _____
$316.70	30/15/3	(9) _____	(10) _____
$ 79.95	30/25/7	(11) _____	(12) _____
$159.50	15/10/2	(13) _____	(14) _____
$335.00	15/10/7	(15) _____	(16) _____
$275.00	40/15/5	(17) _____	(18) _____
$184.50	15/10/3	(19) _____	(20) _____
$293.00	10/15/3	(21) _____	(22) _____
$275.00	18/7½/2	(23) _____	(24) _____
$554.50	20/18/5	(25) _____	(26) _____
$ 99.50	18/15/3	(27) _____	(28) _____
$210.75	25/20/3	(29) _____	(30) _____
$219.50	7½/5½/2	(31) _____	(32) _____
$213.50	5/2½/2	(33) _____	(34) _____
$ 89.50	2½/20/3	(35) _____	(36) _____
$ 72.25	10/10/2	(37) _____	(38) _____
$183.50	15/15/2	(39) _____	(40) _____

INVOICES WITH CASH DISCOUNTS

Example:

15 ea Finger Charts	@ 1.25	=	$18.75
26 ea Flash Card Sets	@ 2.95	=	76.70
6 Boxes Music Paper	@ 3.25	=	19.50
4 Fake Books	@ 12.15	=	48.60
	Sub-total		$163.55
Less 15% Discount			− 24.53
6% Sales Tax			+ 8.43
Shipping Charge			+ 9.88
Return Credit			− 5.38
	Total		$151.86

Solving the Example

STEP 1: Set the Decimal @ 2		
STEP 2: Set Rounding Selector @ 5/4		
Enter	**Depress**	**Notes**
15	☒ X	
1.25	☐ = +	
26	☒ X	
2.95	☐ = +	
6	☒ X	
3.25	☐ = +	
4	☒ X	
12.15	☐ = +	
	☐ ∗	163.55 Subtotal
	☒ X	
15	☐ %	24.53 Discount
	☐ −	139.02 Net amount
	☒ X	
6	☐ %	8.34 Sales tax
	☐ +	147.36 Subtotal
	☐ +	
9.88	☐ +	Shipping charge
5.38	☐ −	Return credit
	☐ ∗	151.86 Amount due

PRACTICE PROBLEMS

INVOICE
NO. 2554

SCOT-ROB PRODUCTIONS
MUSIC & VIDEO
P.O. BOX 68
BELMONT, CA 94002

DATE	
SHIP TO	SAME

SOLD TO: VACAFIELD HIGH SCHOOL
302 MERCURY STREET
FAIRVIEW, CA 92630

ACCOUNT NO.	SALESMAN NO.	PURCHASE ORDER NO.	SHIP VIA	COL	PPD	DATE SHIPPED	TERMS	INVOICE DATE	PAC
6088	20	PR 08281-A	UPS			2-5-XX	N/30	1-28-XX	

QTY. ORDERED	QTY. SHIPPED	QTY. BACK ORDERED	ITEM NO.	DESCRIPTION	UNIT PRICE	DISC. %	EXTENDED PRICE
12	12			BLANK CASSETTE TAPES	1.25		(
22	22			TAPE HEAD CLEANERS	2.95		(
9	9			PADS/MUSIC PAPER	3.25		(
5	5			CASES/VIDEO TAPE	12.15		(
12	12			GUITAR CHORD BKS.	1.97		(
35	35			EASY PIANO BOOKS	2.37		(
8	8			VOCAL SELECTION BOOK	5.68		('
3	3			KEYBOARD CHARTS	1.92		('
						15	('

				SALE AMOUNT	(1
	MISC. CHARGES				
	6% SALES TAX				(1
	FREIGHT			11.89	
THANK YOU	RETURN CREDIT			— 7.65	
	TOTAL				(1

PRACTICE PROBLEMS

SCOT-ROB PRODUCTIONS

MUSIC & VIDEO
P.O. BOX 68
BELMONT, CA 94002

INVOICE
NO. *2565*

SOLD TO: *Sandpoint High School*
2825 Pine Street
Sandpoint, ID 83840

DATE	*2-15-xx*
SHIP TO	*Same*

ACCOUNT NO.	SALESMAN NO.	PURCHASE ORDER NO.	SHIP VIA	COL	PPD	DATE SHIPPED	TERMS	INVOICE DATE	PAGE
2386	*6*	*106258*	*UPS*			*2-15-xx*	*N/30*	*2-6-xx*	

QTY. ORDERED	QTY. SHIPPED	QTY. BACK ORDERED	ITEM NO.	DESCRIPTION	UNIT PRICE	DISC. %	EXTENDED PRICE	
275	*275*			*Holiday Sheet Music*	*.63*			(1)
250	*250*			*Classical Sheet Prints*	*.62*			(2)
45	*45*			*Promotion Music Reprints*	*.67*			(3)
24	*24*			*Golden Tech VHS Video Tape*	*2.15*			(4)
10	*10*			*Pro VHS Video Tape*	*2.96*			(5)
12 Doz.	*12 Doz.*			*Audio Cassettes*	*2.55 Doz.*			(6)
2 RMS	*2 RMS*			*Music Sheets*	*4.72 RM.*			(7)
3 RMS	*3 RMS*			*Deluxe Coated Paper*	*5.05 RM*			(8)
5 RMS	*5 RMS*			*Color Cover Paper*	*4.32 RM*			(9)
						12		(10)

SALE AMOUNT		(11)
MISC. CHARGES	*3.85*	(12)
6% SALES TAX		
FREIGHT	*13.48*	
TOTAL		(13)

THANK YOU

SIMPLE INTEREST

INTEREST is the amount paid or received for the use of money. A common example would be the interest charged for a loan.

Principal = P = amount loaned or borrowed.
Rate   = R = % of interest per year.
Time   = T = number of years or
                     fractions of a year for
                     which the interest is
                     charged.

Formula:

Interest = P × R × T

Example:

Principal	Rate	Time	Interest
$500	17%	90	21.25
	(per year)	(days)	

Convert the 90 days to a year*
and solve the formula.

*A bankers' year = 360 days.

Solving the Example

STEP 1: Set the Decimal @ 2		
STEP 2: Set Rounding Selector @ 5/4		
Enter	**Depress**	**Notes**
500	✕	
.17	✕	
90	÷	
360	=	$21.25 Interest

PRACTICE PROBLEMS

Round all answers to 2 decimal places.

Amount	Rate	Days	Interest
$2758	16%	47	(1) _____
$1648	14%	72	(2) _____
$1564	17%	19	(3) _____
$1328	15%	27	(4) _____
$2847	16%	40	(5) _____
$1450	18%	51	(6) _____
$1763	17%	33	(7) _____
$1974	15%	48	(8) _____
$1827	18%	17	(9) _____
$2761	17%	29	(10) _____
$1645	15%	37	(11) _____
$2564	14%	16	(12) _____
$2027	15%	29	(13) _____
$1374	17%	39	(14) _____
$2124	18%	27	(15) _____

DISCOUNTS ON NOTES

Many businesses often accept promissory notes from their customers. As a result, a business will find itself needing cash to pay bills or buy merchandise. To obtain the needed cash, the business "sells" its notes. This process is called DISCOUNTING. The bank or investor pays the business the MATURITY VALUE less the DISCOUNT. They are happy to do this because they keep the discount and will receive the maturity value of the note on the maturity date. The business is glad to get its money early so it can buy more merchandise to sell therefore earn more profit. The business doesn't receive the full maturity value of the note, but normally the profit it can make on the additional merchandise sales far exceeds the loss of part of the maturity value (the discount).

Formulas:

Interest $= \text{Principal} \times \text{Rate} \times \dfrac{\text{Time}}{360}$

Maturity Value $= \text{Principal} + \text{Interest}$

Discount $= \text{Maturity Value}$
$\times \text{Discount Rate} \times \dfrac{\text{Time}}{360}$

Proceeds $= \text{Maturity Value} - \text{Discount}$

Time in the "Discount" formula is the number of days that the bank has the note.

Solving the Example

STEP 1: Set the Decimal @ 2		
STEP 2: Set Rounding Selector @ 5/4		
Enter	**Depress**	**Notes**
1000	⊞ +	
	⊠ x	
.17	⊠ x	Interest rate
60	÷	
360	= +	28.33 Interest
	◇	1,028.33 Maturity value
	⊠ x	
.18	⊠ x	Discount rate
50	÷	Number of days the bank has the note (60 − 10 = 50)
360	= −	25.71 Discount
	*	1,002.62 Proceeds

Example:

A firm receives a $1,000 note on March 20th, which is due in 60 days with interest at an annual rate of 17%. On March 30th the note is purchased by a bank or investor at a discount rate of 18%. Find the INTEREST, MATURITY VALUE, DISCOUNT, and PROCEEDS.

Principal	**Interest Rate**	**Length of Note**	**Note Date**	10 Days	**Discount Date**
$1,000	17%	60 days	3/20		3/30

Discount Rate	**Interest**	**Maturity Value**	**Discount**	**Proceeds From Bank**
18%	$28.33	$1,028.33	$25.71	$1,002.62

PRACTICE PROBLEMS

Find the (A) Interest, (B) Maturity Value, (C) Discount, and (D) Proceeds. Round all answers to 2 decimal places. Use a 30 day month.

Principal	Interest Rate	Length of Note	Note Date	Discount Date	Discount Rate
(1) $1,150	17%	45 days	1/20	2/10	19%
(2) $1,245	17½%	60 days	9/10	10/15	18%
(3) $1,320	18%	90 days	6/5	6/30	16%
(4) $1,500	19%	120 days	7/6	8/6	17%
(5) $1,600	18½%	80 days	5/10	5/25	18%
(6) $1,750	18%	45 days	4/15	5/5	19%
(7) $1,920	17%	60 days	8/12	9/11	16%
(8) $1,050	16½%	15 days	3/5	3/15	16%
(9) $1,200	17%	70 days	2/5	2/25	17%
(10) $1,820	18%	82 days	10/15	11/5	18%
(11) $1,350	17%	130 days	12/10	12/30	16%
(12) $1,250	18½%	34 days	11/16	11/28	17%
(13) $1,430	16%	20 days	1/5	1/15	16%
(14) $1,500	17%	40 days	2/14	3/6	18%
(15) $2,000	18%	150 days	4/1	6/1	18%

PAYROLL

WAGES

Wages are calculated on a per hour basis. Gross earnings for hourly workers are found by multiplying the hourly rate by the number of hours worked per pay period.

Gross Earnings (wages) $=$ Rate per hour $\times$ number of hours worked.

Example No. 1: A student-aide earns $4.25 per hour. Calculate the gross earnings for a 40-hour work week.

Procedure: Wages $=$ $4.25 $\times$ 40 $=$ $170.00.

OVERTIME

Overtime for employees paid an hourly wage is normally $1\frac{1}{2}$ times the hourly rate for hours worked in excess of a 40-hour work week.

Example No. 2: A receptionist for a metropolitan publishing company earns $4.90 an hour for a 40-hour work week. Calculate her gross earnings for a week in which she worked 48 hours.

Procedure: The overtime rate is $4.90 x 1-1/2 $=$ $7.35. Thus

Regular wages	$=$ $4.90 x 40	$=$	$196.00
Overtime wages	$=$ $7.35 x 8	$=$	58.00
Gross earnings		$=$	$254.80

OVERTIME VARIATIONS

Some wage agreements recognize other forms of overtime. "Time-and-a-half" (one and one-half times the regular rate) may be paid for hours in excess of 8 hours per day, and "double time" (two times the regular rate) is often paid for work on Sundays or holidays.

Example No. 3: The time card of a security guard indicated the following hours worked during the week of Sunday, August 2 through Saturday, August 8. (In this example, the guard's regular work week is Monday through Friday.)

8/2	8/3	8/4	8/5	8/6	8/7	8/8
8	8	10	8½	5	8	0

The regular hourly rate for the employee is $5.40 and he receives time-and-a-half for work in excess of 8 hours a day or 40 hours a week plus double time for Sundays or holidays. Find his gross earnings for the week.

Procedure: The hours worked are distributed as regular (R), overtime or time-and-a-half (OT), and double time (DT).

	8/2	8/3	8/4	8/5	8/6	8/7	8/8	Total Hours	Rate	Total Wages
R		8	8	8	5	8	0	37	$5.40	$199.80
OT			2	½				2½	8.10	20.25
DT	8							8	10.80	86.40
								Gross Earnings		$306.45

PRACTICE PROBLEMS

Find the total wages earned for the following employees. All employees (Nos. 1–10) earn "double time" for working on Sundays and also earn "time-and-a-half" for hours worked in excess of a 40-hour work week. (The regular work week is Monday through Saturday.)

| Em-ployee | TIME RECORD | | | | | | | Rate per hr. | REGULAR EARNINGS | | OVERTIME EARNINGS | | | Total Earnings |
	S	M	T	W	TH	F	S		Hrs.	Amount	Hrs.	Rate	Amount	
1	4	8	8	10	8	8	0	4.00	40	160.00	4 2	8.00 6.00	32.00 12.00	204.00
2	0	8	8	6	7	8	0	4.00						
3	0	6	9	10	8	4	4	4.00						
4	2	8	10	8	7	0	2	4.50						
5	0	6	8	8	8	8	0	4.50						
6	8	4	8	8	4	8	8	4.50						
7	1	8	7	6	10	8	6	5.76						
8	0	10	9	4	9	7	2	5.76						
9	6	0	4	10	5	10		5.76						
10	0	8	6	8	8	4	8	5.80						

SCOT-ROB PRODUCTIONS — TOTAL [ ] — TOTAL [ ]

NET EARNINGS

After the computation of gross earnings, the next step in preparation of the payroll is the calculation of net earnings (gross earnings less employee deductions). Deductions are amounts that are withheld from the employee's earnings by the employer. Social Security with federal and state income taxes are required deductions for most employers. In addition there may be voluntary deductions made by the employer as a service to the employee. Union dues, insurance premiums, U.S. Savings Bonds, retirement and contributions to charitable organizations are examples of such deductions.

F.I.C.A. (Social Security) deductions are 7.51% of the gross pay up to the base (annual limit) of $48,000. When an employee's gross earnings reach the annual limit ($48,000) no additional deductions for FICA will be made in that calendar year.

Example: Calculate the FICA deduction for an employee whose monthly gross pay is $954.82.

Procedure: $954.82 × 7.51% = $71.71

PRACTICE PROBLEMS

For the following February payroll, calculate the FICA deductions. Use the FICA rate 7.51%.

Employee	February Gross Pay	FICA Deduction
1. C. Bradshaw	$1,015.00	$76.23
2. S. Jefferson	863.00	
3. I. Cole	689.53	
4. A. Wong	1,998.06	
5. C. Innis	1,107.70	
TOTAL		

PAYROLL REGISTER

A payroll register is commonly used by the payroll department to organize the data required in computing gross pay, deductions, and net pay.

NOTE: Payroll data must be well organized in order to promote accuracy. Accuracy is of prime importance because mistakes are damaging to employee morale which can easily affect production which in turn can directly affect profits. Errors can also bring penalties to the employer imposed by governmental agencies for incorrect reports.

PRACTICE PROBLEMS

Compute the *total earnings,* and *net pay* on the following payroll register for mid-January. Use the following rates based on the total earnings: FICA—7.51%, city tax—1.25%, pension—6%. All employees receive double the regular rate for hours worked on Sunday. All employees earn 1½ times the regular rate for hours worked in excess of a 40-hour work week. Total all columns where double ruled at the bottom. (The regular work week is Monday through Saturday.)

SCOT-ROB PRODUCTIONS

Payroll Register for 2 Week Period Ending Januay 17, 19xx

Employee No.	M	T	W	Th	F	S	S	M	T	W	Th	F	S	S	Rate Per Hr.	Reg. Hours	Reg. Amount	OT Hours	OT Rate	OT Amount	Total Earnings
*1	8	8	8	8	8	1	0	8	8	8	4	8	4	4	4.25	80	340.00	4 / 1	8.50 / 6.38	34.00 / 6.38	380.38
2	8	8	10	4	8	0	0	8	8	8	8	0	0	0	4.25						
3	8	8	8	8	8	0	0	8	8	8	8	0	0	0	4.25						
4	8	4	0	0	0	4	8	8	4	0	6	0	0	8	6.76						
5	6	6	4	8	8	0	0	4	9	10	0	0	0	0	4.25						
6	9	9	10	8	8	0	2	8	10	4	4	8	2	1	4.80						
7	8	8	8	3	8	2	3	4	11	8	8	0	0	4	4.40						
8	10	10	10	10	0	0	0	8	8	8	0	0	0	8	5.30						
9	8	7	10	8	4	1	4	0	0	2	12	8	4	0	5.30						
10	0	10	11	0	8	5	0	8	8	8	4	6	0	3	4.88						
11	8	9	8	8	7	0	0	8	10	6	0	0	0	0	4.88						
12	8	8	8	8	8	2	4	8	8	8	8	0	0	0	4.88						
13	9	8	10	5	10	0	2	0	8	7	8	8	8	1	4.25						
14	10	10	10	10	0	0	0	10	10	10	10	0	0	0	4.25						
15	8	8	8	8	7	2	0	8	8	8	0	8	0	3	8.20						
16	9	8	8	0	3	10	3	8	8	8	4	4	0	1	8.20						
17	9	9	6	8	0	1	0	9	9	7	10	0	9	4	10.60						
18	9	8	8	6	6	0	4	8	0	8	8	8	8	8	10.60						
19	0	2	8	0	4	0	5	9	9	0	0	0	9	0	4.26						
20	0	9	4	0	0	8	0	0	0	8	9	6	4	8	7.40						

*(Include amounts for employee No. 1 in Totals)

Payroll Register (cont.)

Federal Inc. Tax	State Inc. Tax	F.I.C.A.	City Tax	Pension Fund	Group Insurance	Contribution United Way	Total Deductions	Net Pay	Employee No.
55.80	18.24	28.57	4.75	22.82	3.40	1.00	134.58	245.80	1
48.60	12.02				3.40	2.00			2
49.13	11.89				3.40	1.00			3
97.47	33.71				3.40	3.00			4
37.74	9.20				3.40	–0–			5
47.63	10.01				3.40	1.00			6
51.62	13.19				3.40	1.00			7
35.59	7.11				3.40	1.50			8
68.03	17.34				3.40	2.50			9
47.17	11.91				3.40	2.00			10
41.01	10.45				3.40	1.50			11
38.23	8.78				3.40	–0–			12
26.87	5.17				3.40	–0–			13
29.39	5.95				3.40	–0–			14
81.49	22.32				3.40	2.00			15
94.11	24.86				3.40	2.25			16
119.99	26.61				3.40	3.50			17
136.21	29.91				3.40	1.50			18
52.17	16.08				3.40	–0–			19
70.09	19.71				3.40	1.75			20

Deductions

APPENDIX

PREMACHINE QUIZ

Name: _____ **Date:** _____

DIRECTIONS: Write your answers in the space provided. Perform all your calculations on the Quiz Paper.

(1) Add:
2.46
31.842
7.01
118.2
10.006
_____
_____

(2) Arrange in a column and add:

$3.146 + 20.08 + 3.1 + 701.16 + 20.003 =$ _____

Convert the following fractions into their decimal equivalents.

(3) $\frac{1}{2}$ = _____

(6) $\frac{3}{4}$ = _____

(4) $\frac{1}{4}$ = _____

(7) $\frac{3}{10}$ = _____

(5) $\frac{3}{8}$ = _____

(8) $\frac{2}{5}$ = _____

Add: Convert the fractions to decimals and add.

(9) $2\frac{3}{4} + 6\frac{1}{5} =$ _____

(10) $8\frac{1}{2} + 7\frac{3}{4} + 4\frac{5}{8} + 6\frac{1}{5} =$ _____

Multiply: Convert the fractions to decimals and multiply.

(11) $1\frac{1}{2} \times 2\frac{1}{5} =$ _____

(12) $1\frac{3}{4} \times 12 =$ _____

Indicate the CORRECT DECIMAL PLACEMENT in the product.

			PRODUCT
(13)	$.48 \times 826$	=	39648
(14)	$.037 \times .017$	=	629
(15)	1.8×2.4	=	432
(16)	1.006×3.5	=	35210

PREMACHINE QUIZ (cont.)

(17) Find the total:

2 books at $2.25 each $ _____

3 pens at $.98 each $ _____

TOTAL $ _____

Indicate the CORRECT DECIMAL PLACEMENT in the quotient.

	DIVIDEND		DIVISOR		QUOTIENT
(18)	34.44	÷	246	=	14
(19)	2625	÷	7.5	=	35
(20)	.1995	÷	.019	=	105

CONVERT TO PERCENTS.

(21) 1.18 = _____ %

(22) .50 = _____ %

(23) .5 = _____ %

(24) $3\frac{1}{2}$ = _____ %

(25) .016 = _____ %

CONVERT TO DECIMALS.

(26) 87% = _____

(27) 325% = _____

(28) 8.2% = _____

(29) .25% = _____

(30) 124.4% = _____

DETERMINE THE AMOUNT OF DISCOUNT.

	GROSS AMOUNT	RATE OF DISCOUNT	AMOUNT OF DISCOUNT
(31)	$ 85.00	3%	$ _____
(32)	$ 50.40	2½%	$ _____
(33)	$ 18.00	1%	$ _____
(34)	$100.00	10% and 10%	$ _____

(35) $2.00 is what percent of $4.00? _____ %

(36) $10.00 is what percent more than 8.00? _____ %

(37) $20 is what percent less than $25? _____ %

(38) What percent of $18 is $36? _____ %

(39) $200 plus 10% is what amount? _____

(40) What single rate of discount is equivalent to the discount series 20% and 10%? _____ %

WARMING UP EXERCISES

Try for a column in 15 seconds. (It will take longer on columns 2, 4, 5, 6 and 8.)

(1)	(2)	(3)	(4)	(5)	(6)	(7)	(8)	(9)	(10)
333	666	444	777	888	555	222	999	111	346
313	626	414	717	828	515	242	939	121	220
363	696	484	787	838	535	282	989	131	78
343	636	434	737	848	575	232	919	141	142
393	656	454	767	838	595	262	949	151	382
373	686	424	727	828	565	252	969	161	591
313	676	464	797	818	525	232	989	171	846
323	646	484	717	868	585	212	939	181	29
353	616	434	737	858	545	272	959	191	134
393	626	494	727	848	515	292	969	121	34
363	636	424	767	878	535	282	929	171	722
343	686	474	727	828	595	252	919	161	483
373	626	464	757	898	555	232	949	151	96
393	616	414	737	818	565	262	979	181	122
363	636	434	717	878	545	252	969	131	700
323	626	484	737	828	525	272	929	141	53
343	656	424	767	848	585	212	939	191	202
373	626	464	747	838	535	232	969	151	98
313	686	474	727	828	565	242	919	161	70
353	646	434	737	818	545	262	929	141	535
363	616	414	717	838	525	282	979	151	292
7403	13586	9434	15627	17758	11585	5282	20029	3211	6175

Drill on each of the following numbers:

242	515	102	551	301	141	402	315	205	919

ONE MINUTE PROGRESS GRAPH
(For determining Net and Gross strokes per minute.)

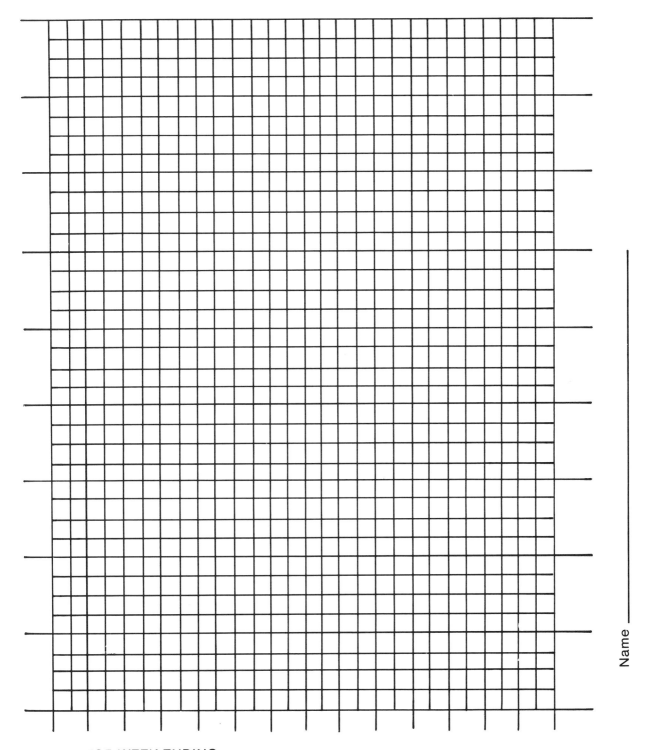

Name

FOR WEEK ENDING—

EIGHT MINUTE PROGRESS GRAPH
(For determining total problems completed and number of errors.)

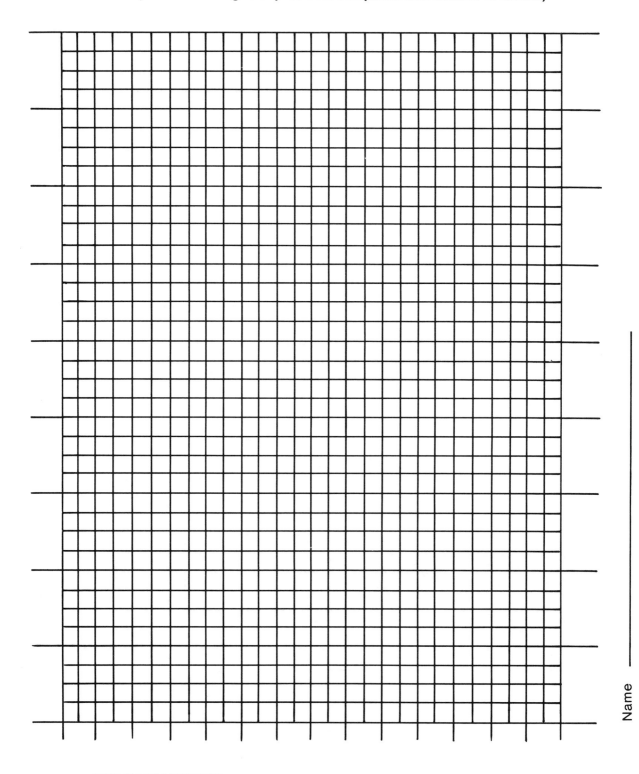

Name

FOR WEEK ENDING—

MID-TERM REVIEW

Addition Problems:

(1)	(2)
2.29	291.32
5.88	695.58
1.09	291.20
9.26	**1,278.10**

(3)	(4)
5.10	426.84
2.21	154.67
6.37	539.98
13.68	**1,121.49**

Subtraction Problems:

(1)	(2)	(3)	(4)
6,245.60	3,203.83 −	95.86 −	24.62
3,178.91 −	4,167.30	32.18 −	81.91 −
3,066.69	**963.47**	47.21	35.75
		59.35 −	256.32 −
		27.77	1.11
		112.41 −	1,022.21 −
			3.74
			1,295.22 −

Multiplication
Whole and Decimal Numbers

Round to 2 decimal places.

(1) $921 \times 23 = 21,183$

(2) $15 \times 122 = 1,830$

(3) $27.6 \times 37.8 = 1,043.28$

(4) $27.5 \times 26 = 715$

(5) $345 \times 9.3 = 3,208.5$

(6) $568 \times 82 = 46,576$

(7) $764 \times 38 = 29,032$

(8) $624 \times 180 = 112,320$

(9) $69.44 \times 1.3 = 90.27$

(10) $41.67 \times 220 = 9,167.4$

Multiple Factors:
Multiplying more than two factors

Round to 2 decimal places.

(1) $15 \times 20 \times 12 = 3,600$

(2) $16 \times 15 \times 3.1 = 744$

(3) $80 \times 19 \times .5 = 760$

(4) $2.25 \times 24 \times 15 = 810$

(5) $52 \times 15 \times 7.2 = 5,616$

(6) $12.4 \times 38 \times 73 = 34,397.6$

(7) $42 \times 8.6 \times 5.7 = 2,058.84$

(8) $54 \times 15 \times 9.5 = 7,695$

(9) $17 \times 53 \times .89 = 801.89$

(10) $91 \times .7 \times 66 = 4,204.2$

(1) 45 lbs. @ \$1.29 per lb. = \$58.05
   6 lbs. @ \$1.29 per lb. = \$7.74
  28 lbs. @ \$1.29 per lb. = \$36.12
  31 lbs. @ \$1.29 per lb. = \$39.99

(2) 28 hats @ \$5.95 each = \$166.60
  73 hats @ \$5.95 each = \$434.35
  39 hats @ \$5.95 each = \$232.05
  46 hats @ \$5.95 each = \$273.70

(3) \$2.60 per hour × 75 hours = \$195.00
  \$2.60 per hour × 80 hours = \$208.00
  \$2.60 per hour × 72 hours = \$187.20
  \$2.60 per hour × 64 hours = \$166.40

Accumulation in Multiplication

(1)

2 lbs. apples @ \$.29/lb.	= \$ .58
4 lbs. grapes @ \$.53/lb.	= \$ 2.12
6 lbs. peaches @ \$.91/lb.	= \$ 5.46
5 lbs. plums @ \$.32/lb.	= \$ 1.60
3 lbs. bananas @ \$.15/lb.	= \$ .45
Total	\$10.21

(2)

60 glasses @ \$.49/glass	= \$ 29.40
48 glasses @ \$.59/glass	= \$ 28.32
32 glasses @ \$.79/glass	= \$ 25.28
24 glasses @ \$.98/glass	= \$ 23.52
89 glasses @ \$.05/glass	= \$ 4.45
Total	\$110.97

(3)

5 yards @ \$4.98/yd.	= \$ 24.90
12 yards @ \$7.98/yd.	= \$ 95.76
3 yards @ \$8.50/yd.	= \$ 25.50
2 yards @ \$4.25/yd.	= \$ 8.50
7 yards @ \$1.98/yd.	= \$ 13.86
Total	\$168.52

Negative Accumulation In Multiplication

Round to 1 decimal place.

(1) $(23 \times 74) - (15 \times 99) = 217$

(2) $(65 \times 68) - (85 \times 54) = -170$

(3) $(46 \times 34) - (88 \times 42) = -2,132$

(4) $(26 \times 74) - (16 \times 66) = 868$

(5) $(35 \times 32) - (45 \times 23) = 85$

(6) $(54 \times 8.7) - (38 \times 6.7) = 215.2$

(7) $(13.3 \times 56) - (9.4 \times 35) = 415.8$

(8) $(6.3 \times 141) - (12.8 \times 36) = 427.5$

(9) $(46 \times 67) - (74 \times 42) = -26$

(10) $(75 \times 8.1) - (34 \times 5.3) = 427.3$

HELP MATE (Problem #1)	
Enter	**Depress**
23	[x]
74	[= +]
15	[x]
99	[= -]
	[*]

Division
With Decimal Answers

Find the quotient rounded to 3 decimal places.

(1) $75,860 \div 548 = 138.431$

(2) $39,827 \div 359 = 110.939$

(3) $70,522 \div 1,095 = 64.404$

(4) $4,473 \div 114 = 39.237$

(5) $11,493 \div 365 = 31.488$

(6) $67,837 \div 865 = 78.424$

(7) $59,632 \div 795 = 75.009$

(8) $10,738 \div 543 = 19.775$

(9) $2,738 \div 46 = 59.522$

(10) $64,580 \div 112 = 576.607$

Division With
Constant Divisor

Find the quotient rounded to 2 decimal places.

(1) $4,592 \div 514 = 8.93$
$2,724 \div 514 = 5.30$
$7,139 \div 514 = 13.89$

(2) $6,418 \div 205 = 31.31$
$12,956 \div 205 = 63.20$
$9,872 \div 205 = 48.16$

(3) $8,416 \div 419 = 20.09$
$16,327 \div 419 = 38.97$
$18,522 \div 419 = 44.21$

(4) $6,672 \div 737 = 9.05$
$2,930 \div 737 = 3.98$
$3,286 \div 737 = 4.46$

(5) $41,590 \div 2,896 = 14.36$
$84,710 \div 2,896 = 29.25$
$20,572 \div 2,896 = 7.10$

Fractions In Operations — Addition

Find the answer rounded to 2 decimal places.

(1)

$$5\frac{1}{3}$$
$$14\frac{2}{7}$$
$$+\ 3\frac{2}{5}$$
$$\overline{23.02}$$

(2)

$$83\frac{4}{5}$$
$$49\frac{2}{3}$$
$$+\ 4\frac{5}{8}$$
$$\overline{138.10}$$

(3)

$$\frac{13}{15}$$
$$3\frac{5}{6}$$
$$+7\frac{2}{8}$$
$$\overline{11.95}$$

Fractions In Operations — Subtraction

Find the answer rounded to 2 decimal places.

(1)

$$427\frac{1}{4}$$
$$168\frac{1}{9}-$$
$$\overline{259.14}$$

(2)

$$570\frac{2}{5}$$
$$316\frac{5}{9}-$$
$$\overline{253.84}$$

(3)

$$928\frac{7}{8}$$
$$288\frac{16}{17}-$$
$$\overline{639.94}$$

Fractions In Operations — Multiplication

Find the answer rounded to 2 decimal places.

(1) $28 \times 32\frac{1}{8} = 899.64$

(2) $17\frac{7}{12} \times 59 = 1{,}037.22$

(3) $62\frac{2}{3} \times 3\frac{7}{8} = 243.16$

Fractions In Operations — Division

Find the answer rounded to 4 decimal places.

(1) $57\frac{1}{3} \div 8 = 7.1667$

(2) $21\frac{1}{4} \div 6\frac{5}{9} = 3.2415$

(3) $321\frac{6}{10} \div 42\frac{2}{3} = 7.5375$

Fractions In Operations — Mixed

Find the answer rounded to 2 decimal places.

(1)

$$35\frac{1}{3}$$
$$112\frac{3}{8}$$
$$+239\frac{1}{14}$$
$$\overline{386.78}$$

(2)

$$512$$
$$16\frac{1}{3}-$$
$$\overline{495.67}$$

(3) $37\frac{1}{8} \times 9\frac{2}{13} = 339.74$

(4) $526\frac{1}{6} \div 13\frac{1}{9} = 40.14$

Addition and Subtraction
Followed by Multiplication or Division

Find the answer rounded to 2 decimal places.

(1) $(242 + 917) \div 113$ = 10.26
(2) $(4,478 - 987) \div 295$ = 11.83
(3) $(14 + 22) \times 47$ = 1,692.00
(4) $(426 - 269) \times 57$ = 8,949.00
(5) $(1,846 - 810) \div 84$ = 12.33
(6) $(412 + 634) \div 89$ = 11.75
(7) $(683 - 417) \times 5.8$ = 1,542.80
(8) $(823 + 506) \times 4.51$ = 5,993.79
(9) $(372 + 290) \div 23$ = 28.78
(10) $(478 + 682) \times 2.8$ = 3,248.00

HELP MATE (Problem #1)	
Enter	**Depress**
242	[+]
917	[+]
	[*]
	[÷]
113	[=]

Multiplication or Division
Followed by Addition and Subtraction

Find the answer rounded to 2 decimal places.

(1) $(23 \times 15) - 125$ = 220.00
(2) $(46 \times 75) + 84$ = 3,534.00
(3) $(1,416 \div 78) + 30$ = 48.15
(4) $(1,889 \div 96) - 10$ = 9.68
(5) $(5,314 \div 82) - 25$ = 39.80
(6) $(46 \times 32) - 473$ = 999.00
(7) $(1,105 \div 45) + 138$ = 162.56
(8) $(68 \times 43) + 398$ = 3,322.00
(9) $(1,898 \div 276) + 859$ = 865.88
(10) $(3,281 \div 57) - 49$ = 8.56

HELP MATE (Problem #1)	
Enter	**Depress**
23	[X]
15	[= +]
125	[−]
	[*]

Multiplication Followed by Division and
Division Followed by Multiplication

Find the answer rounded to 2 decimal places.

(1) $(117 \times 76) \div 225$ = 39.52
(2) $(9,636.16 \div 32) \times 32$ = 352.00
(3) $(24 \times 71) \div 112$ = 15.21
(4) $(87 \times 44) \div 16$ = 239.25
(5) $(9,050 \div 362) \times 12$ = 300.00
(6) $(92 \times 17) \div 41$ = 38.15
(7) $(4,897 \div 83) \times 28$ = 1,652.00
(8) $(3,289 \div 115) \times 91$ = 2,602.60
(9) $(126 \times 46) \div 187$ = 30.99
(10) $(63,600 \div 900) \times 45$ = 3,180.00

HELP MATE (Problem #1)	
Enter	**Depress**
117	[X]
76	[÷]
225	[=]

Percentage

A. Find the percentage of a number.   P = Percentage

B. Find what percent one number is of another   R = Rate Percent

C. Find the base, or the 100% number.   B = Base

Then find the answer to the problem rounded to 2 decimal places.

  (1) 680 (P) is _____ % of 5,823 (B)?   11.68% = (R)

  (2) 89% (R) of 962 (B) = _____ ?   856.18 = (P)

  (3) 139 (P) is 51.2% (R) of _____ ?   271.48 = (B)

  (4) 492 (P) is _____ % of 3,021 (B)?   16.29% = (R)

  (5) 837 (P) is _____ % of 6,281 (B)?   13.33% = (R)

  (6) 937 (P) is 23% (R) of _____ ?   4,073.91 = (B)

  (7) 33% (R) of 9,182 (B) = _____ ?   3,030.06 = (P)

  (8) 19% (R) of 2,910 (B) = _____ ?   552.90 = (P)

  (9) 1,735 (P) is 46.1% (R) of _____ ?   3,763.56 = (B)

(10) 58.5% (R) of 499 (B) = _____ ?   291.92 = (P)

HELP MATE

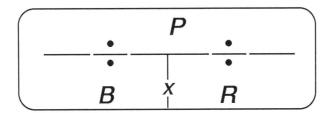

NOTE: See page 4 for arithmetic review.

ELECTRONIC CALCULATOR REVIEW FOR FINAL EXAM
PART I — Addition

Add for 8 minutes and stop immediately. Answers will be taken from the tape.

(1)	(2)	(3)	(4)	(5)
64.80	4.67	5.87	4.09	39.75
20.16	.12	44.12	97.59	27.61
9.41	63.77	5.11	5.43	1.16
108.78	2.25	8.43	50.60	1.23
4.75	37.08	.60	2.66	23.30
51.90	9.55	31.65	61.59	4.05
8.87	32.76	9.04	2.42	.87
6.32	.27	2.01	10.09	8.46
4.91	26.15	58.75	9.83	23.08
8.79	9.07	.85	5.08	42.55
70.48	.86	5.07	2.46	80.43
8.53	34.33	9.65	14.07	1.99

(6)	(7)	(8)	(9)	(10)
4.01	9.41	90.47	6.66	2.13
3.74	6.04	21.38	30.85	5.73
2.67	5.85	7.04	5.33	7.95
1.25	40.81	31.54	.90	4.25
9.40	52.44	5.00	7.62	5.06
38.80	7.07	35.90	.20	10.02
26.83	580.41	50.59	9.08	8.56
9.05	59.52	5.39	1.25	40.95
15.96	9.17	23.68	11.76	.35
89.65	12.56	30.97	165.74	4.14
34.92	.97	31.32	4.31	54.33
6.29	6.65	8.43	6.22	6.39

(11)	(12)	(13)	(14)	(15)
5.44	19.53	68.28	54.73	6.35
15.06	.23	6.04	351.86	112.48
30.39	.22	10.56	1.06	68.03
65.44	30.11	8.06	9.71	9.56
61.33	2.08	13.08	10.01	.50
17.58	1.49	5.56	263.89	2.06
7.09	146.49	1.40	95.07	2.20
10.51	52.47	36.65	4.25	60.81
34.29	5.98	70.54	1.97	2.19
42.27	2.75	100.47	72.73	7.04
42.77	.93	7.13	91.58	.85
65.09	6.39	17.85	24.98	5.53

PART I — Addition (cont.)

Add for 8 minutes and stop immediately. Answers will be taken from the tape.

(16)	(17)	(18)	(19)	(20)
9.38	3.30	73.54	4.22	54.88
39.54	17.60	3.44	.21	4.65
40.08	862.15	65.90	9.52	6.55
1.91	17.64	64.36	50.58	90.87
1.66	9.05	7.10	35.07	76.75
80.50	7.77	5.06	3.52	6.87
65.04	5.21	501.43	31.73	60.02
1.61	10.59	8.20	1.08	50.42
15.64	80.51	9.85	49.16	4.09
9.08	61.98	72.38	.98	65.95
42.85	70.04	.19	43.29	804.56
3.26	3.29	6.48	60.39	58.11

(21)	(22)	(23)	(24)	(25)
44.10	68.63	628.67	66.03	65.43
528.21	9.09	138.51	102.00	95.62
206.60	553.72	407.64	547.31	5.42
180.86	905.01	53.21	44.42	82.23
504.41	34.41	67.45	303.05	77.13
165.41	420.11	94.18	52.10	99.12
520.77	37.92	723.05	621.85	98.22
305.46	805.52	77.00	32.65	95.19
925.42	249.97	31.88	90.62	809.32
491.03	28.34	709.85	651.86	64.16
831.59	69.45	487.12	508.94	775.33
353.10	80.00	99.74	31.85	64.76

(26)	(27)	(28)	(29)	(30)
34.51	505.17	68.09	49.23	83.36
502.33	64.01	40.32	575.10	196.39
66.41	721.25	801.05	430.87	372.15
840.67	59.44	26.00	109.15	319.52
10.59	193.06	450.08	327.95	39.75
25.09	245.12	608.90	608.70	750.89
501.07	310.47	383.09	137.98	42.07
206.86	2.30	436.29	26.37	301.05
984.55	169.53	45.26	519.96	838.44
75.08	851.65	579.26	405.48	46.52
459.82	757.52	51.17	99.04	557.93
7.04	66.79	81.35	61.43	4.06

PART II — Calculations

DIRECTIONS:

1. Round dollars and cents answers to the nearest cent.
2. Indicate CREDIT BALANCES as such.
   Credit amounts not so labeled will be counted as incorrect.
3. For percent answers, calculations should be rounded at the fourth decimal place.
4. For answers that are not percent or dollars, give the most possible number of decimal places unless otherwise directed.
5. Record your answers in the ANSWERS COLUMN.

PERFORM THE CALCULATIONS REQUIRED

(1)
```
   .076234
   .0032
   .00265
   .0000088
   .09
   .06234
```

(2)
```
    52.45
  − 77.85
```

(3) $72 \times 55.48 =$

(4) $29 \times 46.328 =$

(5) $29 \times 2745.55 =$

(6) $45.2 \times 6.8 \times 53.98 =$

---

(7) $95.2 \times 786 =$
(8) $.93 \times 53 =$
(9) $2.22 \times 478 =$
(10) Total =

---

(11) $(49 \times 51) + (582 \times 4.2) + (65.1 \times 9.7) =$

ROUND PROBLEMS TO 4 DECIMALS

(12) a.) $520711 \div 4869 =$
   b.) $620598 \div 4869 =$
   c.) $612421 \div 4869 =$

(13) $281\frac{2}{5}$
   $\times 8\frac{3}{16}$

(14) What is 71% of 687?
(15) 626.93 is 22.30% of ?
(16) What % of 4337.98 is 2624.02?

Previous Year	Present Year	Amount of Change	Percent Change
$5,318.62	$4,937.51	(17) _____	(18) _____
4,621.38	3,816.54	(19) _____	(20) _____
9,857.42	7,861.87	(21) _____	(22) _____

COMPUTE THE PERCENT OF SALES FOR EACH DEPT.

Dept.	Sales	Percent
A	$524.52	(24) _____
B	433.43	(25) _____
C	641.83	(26) _____
Total (23)		100%

ANSWERS

1. _____
2. _____
3. _____
4. _____
5. _____
6. _____
7. _____
8. _____
9. _____
10. _____
11. _____
12. a. _____
   b. _____
   c. _____
13. _____
14. _____
15. _____
16. _____
17. _____
18. _____
19. _____
20. _____
21. _____
22. _____
23. _____
24. _____
25. _____
26. _____

INVOICE

Quantity	Unit Price	Extension
17	$ 5.31	(27) _____
9	16.94	(28) _____
8	59.37	(29) _____
12	5.82	(30) _____
45	.65	(31) _____
	Sub Total	(32) _____
	Sales Tax–6%	(33) _____
	TOTAL	(34) _____

CHAIN DISCOUNTS

List Price	% Discount	Amount Discount	Net Amount
$595.00	25–20–5	(35) _____	(36) _____
995.68	35–25–15	(37) _____	(38) _____

SIMPLE INTEREST (USE 360)

Amount	Rate	Days	Interest
7250	7%	58	(39) _____
4666	9%	88	(40) _____

MARKUP BASED ON SELLING PRICE

(41) What is the selling price if the cost is $21.75 and the markup is 40%?

(42) What is the cost if the selling price is $35.00 and the markup is 35%?

DISCOUNTS

Find the (a) interest, (b) maturity value, (c) discount, and (d) proceeds. Round answers to 2 decimal places.

Value of Note	% Rate	Length of Note	Note Date	Discount Date	Discount Rate	
250	7	45 days	1/15	2/5	9	(43)
795	8	88 days	2/13	3/15	6	(44)

ANSWERS

27. _____

28. _____

29. _____

30. _____

31. _____

32. _____

33. _____

34. _____

35. _____

36. _____

37. _____

38. _____

39. _____

40. _____

41. _____

42. _____

43. a. _____

    b. _____

    c. _____

    d. _____

44. a. _____

    h _____

    c. _____

    d. _____

GLOSSARY OF COMMON BUSINESS TERMS

Account: A business record showing amounts paid and owed.

Accounts payable: Bills owed to others.

Accounts receivable: Total bills to be collected from others.

Accrue: To grow, to be added to, to mature.

Accumulative multiplication: The sum of two or more products or the sum of one or more products and a previously known number.

Adjust: Put in order, regulate, or make a settlement.

Adjusted balance: Actual amount available in a checking account at a particular point in time.

Aggregate: Total sum, quantity, or number of anything.

Algorithm: A fixed, step-by-step procedure designed to lead to the solution of a problem.

Allocate: Assign or allot.

Allotment: A share, part, or portion, granted or distributed.

Amortizing: Paying off a loan in monthly payments.

Analysis: Careful study of a problem, or the method of finding a solution or a better way.

Annual: Yearly, coming every year.

Annuity: A sum paid to another party for a period of years; an equal periodic payment.

Approximate: Come close to; not exact; about.

Ascertain: Find out by trial, examination, or experiment, so as to know for certain; determine.

Assessment: Value put on property for tax purposes.

Assets: Possessions of value; all things a business owns or has owed to it.

Audit: Examine or check records, inventory, or other data.

Bad debts: Money owed by a customer unwilling or unable to pay.

Balance: Make things equal.

Balance due: Amount owed.

Balance sheet: A financial report presenting a complete picture of the financial condition of a business on a particular date.

Base: Basis of comparison, the number of which so many hundredths is taken.

Beneficiary: Person or organization that will receive the financial benefits of a life insurance policy.

Bill of lading: A receipt issued by a transport company, with copies going to sender of goods and to receiver.

Bill of sale: A document transferring title in personal property from seller to buyer.

Bills: Statements of money owed for work done, things supplied, or service provided.

Book value: Estimated worth of a fixed asset, as shown by the records. Different from actual or marketable value.

Budget: An estimate of expected income and expense, or of operating results, for a given period in the future.

Cancel: With fractions, eliminating a common divisor from numerator and denominator; removing equivalent values from both sides of an equation.

Cash: Currency, checks, money orders.

Cash discount: A reduction in the price of merchandise offered to a buyer for early payment.

Chain discount: A method of price adjustment based on a series of discounts, each discount being taken on the net price after the preceding discount has been deducted.

Check: A written order instructing a banker to pay a certain amount of money out of a particular account.

Chip: In a calculator, the integrated electronic circuitry that transforms what is entered on a keyboard into a displayed answer. A chip is very small and does the job of what formerly took many thousands of transistors.

Co-insurance: Policy holder and insurance company share the financial loss of property damage.

Commission: A sum of money allowed an agent for services rendered.

Common carrier: A transportation firm authorized by the federal government to carry freight over established routes on established schedules and at approved rates.

Compensation: Something given or received as an equivalent for services, debt, loss, suffering; an indemnity.

Complement: Difference between a number and the next higher power of ten.

Complex fraction: A fraction with a mixed number in the numerator or denominator or both.

Compound interest: Interest that is earned on interest and redeposited or credited to an account at the end of a conversion period.

Computation: Reaching a solution by adding, subtracting, dividing, or multiplying.

Computer: A machine that accepts instructions and information and which follows the instructions to perform operations on the information.

Constant: A numerical value that remains unchanged during a given period or during a series of calculations.

Constant function: On a calculator, a device for locking in a number used in successive calculations, to avoid re-entering the number each time it is used. Most constant functions work for both multiplication and division.

Contract carrier: An independent transport firm that has negotiable rates, schedules, and routes.

Cost: Amount paid.

Credit: Payment over time for goods or services sold on trust; the balance in a person's favor in an account. In customer accounts, a reduction.

Credit balance: Total result of over-subtracting; a negative balance.

Credit memorandum: A paper showing credit on account.

Creditor: Person or company to whom money is owed.

Cross-footing: Adding a column or columns vertically, after computing horizontally; provides a check of calculation accuracy.

CWT: Hundredweight, or 100 pounds; indicates that a weight given is in units of 100 pounds.

Debit: In customer accounts, a charge.

Debtor: Person or company owing money.

Decimal equivalent: Number in decimal form resulting from the division of the numerator of a fraction by the denominator.

Decimal point: A period distinguishing whole numbers (written to the left) from decimal fractions (written to the right).

Decimal point, floating and fixed: A floating decimal point in an electronic calculator automatically moves the decimal to the correct position in an answer. If set to a fixed decimal position, the calculator drops all but the significant decimal digits; if it has automatic round-off, the calculator rounds the displayed answer.

Denominator: The part of a common fraction written below the line; indicates the number of equal parts into which the whole has been divided.

Depreciation: A decrease in value due to wear, decay, age, or obsolescence.

Digit: Any of the integers from 0 through 9.

Discount: A deduction allowed from the face amount of an invoice for a certain consideration, such as cash payment or quantity purchase; interest deducted in advance from the proceeds of a loan.

Discounting: Purchase of a negotiable note due in the future, for a sum smaller than the face value of the note.

Dividend: Number that is to be divided by another.

Dividends: Profits distributed to shareholder-owners of a corporation.

Divisor: Number by which to divide.

Double multiplication: Machine multiplication of two numbers by another number to give two products simultaneously.

Endorsement: Signature of the payee on the back of a check.

Escrow account: An account kept by a lending institution into which a borrower pays in order to accumulate money enough to pay property taxes and property insurance when they come due.

Exemptions: For income tax purposes, the legal dependents and employees claimed by an employer to reduce the amount of tax withheld.

Extension: The product of multiplying two factors, as in extending an invoice. Quantity times price equals extension.

F.O.B. (Free On Board): When merchandise is placed on a transport vehicle free of charge.

Face value: Original amount of a loan.

Flowchart: A graphic representation of a computer program in which symbols represent operations.

Fraction: A way of expressing division or a ratio, in which one number (numerator) is above a line, and another number (denominator) is below the line. See also **Complex fraction, Improper fraction, Mixed number,** and **Proper fraction.**

Gross: Twelve dozen (or 144) items; overall total before deductions.

Gross earnings: Amount earned by an employee in a pay period.

Improper fraction: A fraction in which the numerator is larger than the denominator; value is always greater than one.

Income statement: A report showing the financial activity of a firm over a period of time.

Inflation: A general increase in the prices of most goods and services.

Installment: A partial payment.

Interest: Any payment made for the use of capital.

Inventory: A detailed list of articles with number and value of each.

Invoice: An itemized bill sent to a buyer, containing the prices that comprise the total charge.

Itemize: Make a list of items.

:Liabilities Things of value that a business owes to others; debts.

Liquidate: Discharge, pay off, convert into cash by selling.

List price: Price shown in a catalog, often subject to trade discounts.

Lowest common denominator (LCD): Smallest whole number that is divisible, without a remainder, by all the denominators in a series of fractions. Addition or subtraction of fractions having different denominators is simplified by converting each fraction to its equivalent in terms of the LCD.

Margin: Difference between cost and selling price.

Mark down: Lower the prices on overstocked or out-of-style goods in order to sell them faster.

Mark up: Add to the price of goods an amount to cover costs and profit. Cost plus mark up equals retail selling price.

Maturity: Due date of a loan.

Maturity value: Loan principal plus interest.

Mean: Arithmetic average of a data set.

Median: Middle-ranked value of a data set.

Merchandise: Goods bought for resale.

Mill: Monetary value equal to 1/1,000 of a dollar.

Minuend: A number from which another is to be subtracted.

Mixed number: A fraction consisting of a whole number and a proper fraction.

Multiplicand: A number being multiplied by another number.

Multiplier: A number by which one multiplies.

Mode: Most frequently occurring value in a data set.

Nanosecond: One thousandth of a millionth of a second.

Negative multiplication: Subtraction of one product from another or from any previously known number.

Negotiable instrument: A written paper, signed by a maker or drawer, containing a promise or order to pay a sum of money, which is transferable.

Net: That which remains after deducting all charges, outlay, or loss.

Net: That which remains after deducting all charges, outlay, or loss.

Net income: Profit after all expenses and taxes.

Net purchases: Total amount of purchases less the amount of returned goods.

Net sales: Total amount of sales minus discount allowances and net returns.

Net worth: Total value of a business after all debts have been deducted.

Note: A written promise to pay a definite sum of money on demand or at a specified time.

Numerator: That part of a proper fraction written above the line, indicating the number of equal parts of the whole represented by the fraction.

Overhead: Expenses of managing a business.

Overtime: Time worked by an employee in addition to regular work time.

Payee: Person to whom a check is payable.

Payment: Thing given in discharge of a debt.

Percent: Literally, parts of 100.

Policy: A contractual document explaining the financial commitment of an insurance company to a policy holder.

Premium: A payment amount for insurance protection.

Present value: Amount which, when compounded at a given rate per period, will total a desired sum at a future date.

Principal: Quantity of money borrowed on which interest is calculated.

Proceeds: In bank discount procedure, the amount received when a negotiable note is endorsed and exchanged for cash.

Product: Result of multiplication.

Program: A set of computer instructions.

Proper fraction: A fraction in which the numerator is smaller than the denominator; value is always less than one.

Prorate: To divide or distribute proportionally.

:Quotient Result of division.

Rate: Percent or parts of 100, applied against a base amount or figure.

Ratio: A relationship expressed in numbers. Examples: 2 to 1, or 2:1, or 2/1.

Reciprocal: Quotient resulting from dividing 1 by a given number.

Remit: Give or send payment.

Remittance: Payment of an amount due.

Sales allowance: Adjustments made in the price of merchandise to compensate the buyer for keeping the damaged or wrong merchandise.

Service charge: A charge to a depositor by a bank for use of an account, for imprinting of checks, or for other services.

Simulation: Using a computer program as a model of a real-life situation.

Sinking fund: The accumulation of payments in an interest-paying investment to ensure a desired amount at a future date.

Software: A computer's programs, plus the procedure for their use.

Subroutine: A computer program called for as part of a larger program.

Subtrahend: A number to be subtracted from another number.

Sum: The result of adding two or more numbers.

Tare: Allowance made for the weight of a merchandise container; weight of a vehicle without its load.

Term of note: Number of days between the date of a note and its due date.

Trade discount: A reduction in list price for quantity purchase or for the assumption of marketing functions by the buyer.

Turnover: Number of times the average inventory is sold. A measure of success for the retailer.

Variable: A value that changes with each problem. The opposite of a variable is a constant.

Verify: Prove as true.

Name _____

Class Hour _____

Page _____

No.　　Answer

___　　_____

___　　_____

___　　_____

___　　_____

___　　_____

___　　_____

___　　_____

___　　_____

___　　_____

___　　_____

___　　_____

___　　_____

___　　_____

___　　_____

___　　_____

___　　_____

___　　_____

___　　_____

___　　_____

___　　_____

___　　_____

___　　_____

___　　_____

___　　_____

___　　_____

___　　_____

___　　_____

___　　_____

___　　_____

___　　_____

___　　_____

___　　_____

Name _____

Class Hour _____

Page _____

No.　　Answer

___　　_____

___　　_____

___　　_____

___　　_____

___　　_____

___　　_____

___　　_____

___　　_____

___　　_____

___　　_____

___　　_____

___　　_____

___　　_____

___　　_____

___　　_____

___　　_____

___　　_____

___　　_____

___　　_____

___　　_____

___　　_____

___　　_____

___　　_____

___　　_____

___　　_____

___　　_____

___　　_____

___　　_____

___　　_____

___　　_____

___　　_____

___　　_____

Name _____

Class Hour _____

Page _____

No.　　Answer

___　　_____

___　　_____

___　　_____

___　　_____

___　　_____

___　　_____

___　　_____

___　　_____

___　　_____

___　　_____

___　　_____

___　　_____

___　　_____

___　　_____

___　　_____

___　　_____

___　　_____

___　　_____

___　　_____

___　　_____

___　　_____

___　　_____

___　　_____

___　　_____

___　　_____

___　　_____

___　　_____

___　　_____

___　　_____

___　　_____

___　　_____

___　　_____

Name ———————————

Class Hour ———————

Page ——————————

No.   Answer

——— ———————
——— ———————
——— ———————
——— ———————
——— ———————
——— ———————
——— ———————
——— ———————
——— ———————
——— ———————
——— ———————
——— ———————
——— ———————
——— ———————
——— ———————
——— ———————
——— ———————
——— ———————
——— ———————
——— ———————
——— ———————
——— ———————
——— ———————
——— ———————
——— ———————
——— ———————
——— ———————
——— ———————
——— ———————
——— ———————
——— ———————

Name ———————————

Class Hour ———————

Page ——————————

No.   Answer

——— ———————
——— ———————
——— ———————
——— ———————
——— ———————
——— ———————
——— ———————
——— ———————
——— ———————
——— ———————
——— ———————
——— ———————
——— ———————
——— ———————
——— ———————
——— ———————
——— ———————
——— ———————
——— ———————
——— ———————
——— ———————
——— ———————
——— ———————
——— ———————
——— ———————
——— ———————
——— ———————
——— ———————
——— ———————
——— ———————
——— ———————

Name ———————————

Class Hour ———————

Page ——————————

No.   Answer

——— ———————
——— ———————
——— ———————
——— ———————
——— ———————
——— ———————
——— ———————
——— ———————
——— ———————
——— ———————
——— ———————
——— ———————
——— ———————
——— ———————
——— ———————
——— ———————
——— ———————
——— ———————
——— ———————
——— ———————
——— ———————
——— ———————
——— ———————
——— ———————
——— ———————
——— ———————
——— ———————
——— ———————
——— ———————
——— ———————
——— ———————

Name _____

Class Hour _____

Page _____

No.   Answer

_____ _____
_____ _____
_____ _____
_____ _____
_____ _____
_____ _____
_____ _____
_____ _____
_____ _____
_____ _____
_____ _____
_____ _____
_____ _____
_____ _____
_____ _____
_____ _____
_____ _____
_____ _____
_____ _____
_____ _____
_____ _____
_____ _____
_____ _____
_____ _____
_____ _____
_____ _____
_____ _____
_____ _____
_____ _____
_____ _____
_____ _____
_____ _____
_____ _____

Name _____

Class Hour _____

Page _____

No.   Answer

_____ _____
_____ _____
_____ _____
_____ _____
_____ _____
_____ _____
_____ _____
_____ _____
_____ _____
_____ _____
_____ _____
_____ _____
_____ _____
_____ _____
_____ _____
_____ _____
_____ _____
_____ _____
_____ _____
_____ _____
_____ _____
_____ _____
_____ _____
_____ _____
_____ _____
_____ _____
_____ _____
_____ _____
_____ _____
_____ _____
_____ _____
_____ _____
_____ _____

Name _____

Class Hour _____

Page _____

No.   Answer

_____ _____
_____ _____
_____ _____
_____ _____
_____ _____
_____ _____
_____ _____
_____ _____
_____ _____
_____ _____
_____ _____
_____ _____
_____ _____
_____ _____
_____ _____
_____ _____
_____ _____
_____ _____
_____ _____
_____ _____
_____ _____
_____ _____
_____ _____
_____ _____
_____ _____
_____ _____
_____ _____
_____ _____
_____ _____
_____ _____
_____ _____
_____ _____
_____ _____

Name		Name		Name	
Class Hour		Class Hour		Class Hour	
Page		Page		Page	
No.	Answer	No.	Answer	No.	Answer

Name _____

Class Hour _____

Page _____

No.   Answer

_____ _____
_____ _____
_____ _____
_____ _____
_____ _____
_____ _____
_____ _____
_____ _____
_____ _____
_____ _____
_____ _____
_____ _____
_____ _____
_____ _____
_____ _____
_____ _____
_____ _____
_____ _____
_____ _____
_____ _____
_____ _____
_____ _____
_____ _____
_____ _____
_____ _____
_____ _____
_____ _____
_____ _____
_____ _____

Name _____

Class Hour _____

Page _____

No.   Answer

_____ _____
_____ _____
_____ _____
_____ _____
_____ _____
_____ _____
_____ _____
_____ _____
_____ _____
_____ _____
_____ _____
_____ _____
_____ _____
_____ _____
_____ _____
_____ _____
_____ _____
_____ _____
_____ _____
_____ _____
_____ _____
_____ _____
_____ _____
_____ _____
_____ _____
_____ _____
_____ _____
_____ _____
_____ _____

Name _____

Class Hour _____

Page _____

No.   Answer

_____ _____
_____ _____
_____ _____
_____ _____
_____ _____
_____ _____
_____ _____
_____ _____
_____ _____
_____ _____
_____ _____
_____ _____
_____ _____
_____ _____
_____ _____
_____ _____
_____ _____
_____ _____
_____ _____
_____ _____
_____ _____
_____ _____
_____ _____
_____ _____
_____ _____
_____ _____
_____ _____
_____ _____
_____ _____

Name _____

Class Hour _____

Page _____

No.	Answer
___	_____
___	_____
___	_____
___	_____
___	_____
___	_____
___	_____
___	_____
___	_____
___	_____
___	_____
___	_____
___	_____
___	_____
___	_____
___	_____
___	_____
___	_____
___	_____
___	_____
___	_____
___	_____
___	_____
___	_____
___	_____
___	_____
___	_____
___	_____
___	_____
___	_____

Name _____

Class Hour _____

Page _____

No.	Answer
___	_____
___	_____
___	_____
___	_____
___	_____
___	_____
___	_____
___	_____
___	_____
___	_____
___	_____
___	_____
___	_____
___	_____
___	_____
___	_____
___	_____
___	_____
___	_____
___	_____
___	_____
___	_____
___	_____
___	_____
___	_____
___	_____
___	_____
___	_____
___	_____
___	_____

Name _____

Class Hour _____

Page _____

No.	Answer
___	_____
___	_____
___	_____
___	_____
___	_____
___	_____
___	_____
___	_____
___	_____
___	_____
___	_____
___	_____
___	_____
___	_____
___	_____
___	_____
___	_____
___	_____
___	_____
___	_____
___	_____
___	_____
___	_____
___	_____
___	_____
___	_____
___	_____
___	_____
___	_____
___	_____

Name _____

Class Hour _____

Page _____

No.	Answer
____	_____
____	_____
____	_____
____	_____
____	_____
____	_____
____	_____
____	_____
____	_____
____	_____
____	_____
____	_____
____	_____
____	_____
____	_____
____	_____
____	_____
____	_____
____	_____
____	_____
____	_____
____	_____
____	_____
____	_____
____	_____
____	_____
____	_____
____	_____
____	_____
____	_____
____	_____

Name _____

Class Hour _____

Page _____

No.	Answer
____	_____
____	_____
____	_____
____	_____
____	_____
____	_____
____	_____
____	_____
____	_____
____	_____
____	_____
____	_____
____	_____
____	_____
____	_____
____	_____
____	_____
____	_____
____	_____
____	_____
____	_____
____	_____
____	_____
____	_____
____	_____
____	_____
____	_____
____	_____
____	_____
____	_____
____	_____

Name _____

Class Hour _____

Page _____

No.	Answer
____	_____
____	_____
____	_____
____	_____
____	_____
____	_____
____	_____
____	_____
____	_____
____	_____
____	_____
____	_____
____	_____
____	_____
____	_____
____	_____
____	_____
____	_____
____	_____
____	_____
____	_____
____	_____
____	_____
____	_____
____	_____
____	_____
____	_____
____	_____
____	_____
____	_____
____	_____

Name _____

Class Hour _____

Page _____

No.   Answer

_____   _____
_____   _____
_____   _____
_____   _____
_____   _____
_____   _____
_____   _____
_____   _____
_____   _____
_____   _____
_____   _____
_____   _____
_____   _____
_____   _____
_____   _____
_____   _____
_____   _____
_____   _____
_____   _____
_____   _____
_____   _____
_____   _____
_____   _____
_____   _____
_____   _____
_____   _____
_____   _____
_____   _____
_____   _____
_____   _____
_____   _____

Name _____

Class Hour _____

Page _____

No.   Answer

_____   _____
_____   _____
_____   _____
_____   _____
_____   _____
_____   _____
_____   _____
_____   _____
_____   _____
_____   _____
_____   _____
_____   _____
_____   _____
_____   _____
_____   _____
_____   _____
_____   _____
_____   _____
_____   _____
_____   _____
_____   _____
_____   _____
_____   _____
_____   _____
_____   _____
_____   _____
_____   _____
_____   _____
_____   _____
_____   _____
_____   _____

Name _____

Class Hour _____

Page _____

No.   Answer

_____   _____
_____   _____
_____   _____
_____   _____
_____   _____
_____   _____
_____   _____
_____   _____
_____   _____
_____   _____
_____   _____
_____   _____
_____   _____
_____   _____
_____   _____
_____   _____
_____   _____
_____   _____
_____   _____
_____   _____
_____   _____
_____   _____
_____   _____
_____   _____
_____   _____
_____   _____
_____   _____
_____   _____
_____   _____
_____   _____
_____   _____

Name _____

Class Hour _____

Page _____

No.   Answer

___ _____
___ _____
___ _____
___ _____
___ _____
___ _____
___ _____
___ _____
___ _____
___ _____
___ _____
___ _____
___ _____
___ _____
___ _____
___ _____
___ _____
___ _____
___ _____
___ _____
___ _____
___ _____
___ _____
___ _____
___ _____
___ _____
___ _____
___ _____
___ _____
___ _____
___ _____
___ _____
___ _____

Name _____

Class Hour _____

Page _____

No.   Answer

___ _____
___ _____
___ _____
___ _____
___ _____
___ _____
___ _____
___ _____
___ _____
___ _____
___ _____
___ _____
___ _____
___ _____
___ _____
___ _____
___ _____
___ _____
___ _____
___ _____
___ _____
___ _____
___ _____
___ _____
___ _____
___ _____
___ _____
___ _____
___ _____
___ _____
___ _____
___ _____
___ _____

Name _____

Class Hour _____

Page _____

No.   Answer

___ _____
___ _____
___ _____
___ _____
___ _____
___ _____
___ _____
___ _____
___ _____
___ _____
___ _____
___ _____
___ _____
___ _____
___ _____
___ _____
___ _____
___ _____
___ _____
___ _____
___ _____
___ _____
___ _____
___ _____
___ _____
___ _____
___ _____
___ _____
___ _____
___ _____
___ _____
___ _____
___ _____

Name _____   Name _____   Name _____

Class Hour _____   Class Hour _____   Class Hour _____

Page _____   Page _____   Page _____

No.   Answer   No.   Answer   No.   Answer

____ _____   ____ _____   ____ _____

____ _____   ____ _____   ____ _____

____ _____   ____ _____   ____ _____

____ _____   ____ _____   ____ _____

____ _____   ____ _____   ____ _____

____ _____   ____ _____   ____ _____

____ _____   ____ _____   ____ _____

____ _____   ____ _____   ____ _____

____ _____   ____ _____   ____ _____

____ _____   ____ _____   ____ _____

____ _____   ____ _____   ____ _____

____ _____   ____ _____   ____ _____

____ _____   ____ _____   ____ _____

____ _____   ____ _____   ____ _____

____ _____   ____ _____   ____ _____

____ _____   ____ _____   ____ _____

____ _____   ____ _____   ____ _____

____ _____   ____ _____   ____ _____

____ _____   ____ _____   ____ _____

____ _____   ____ _____   ____ _____

____ _____   ____ _____   ____ _____

____ _____   ____ _____   ____ _____

____ _____   ____ _____   ____ _____

____ _____   ____ _____   ____ _____

____ _____   ____ _____   ____ _____

____ _____   ____ _____   ____ _____

____ _____   ____ _____   ____ _____

____ _____   ____ _____   ____ _____

____ _____   ____ _____   ____ _____

____ _____   ____ _____   ____ _____

Name _____

Class Hour _____

Page _____

No.   Answer

___ _____
___ _____
___ _____
___ _____
___ _____
___ _____
___ _____
___ _____
___ _____
___ _____
___ _____
___ _____
___ _____
___ _____
___ _____
___ _____
___ _____
___ _____
___ _____
___ _____
___ _____
___ _____
___ _____
___ _____
___ _____
___ _____
___ _____
___ _____
___ _____

Name _____

Class Hour _____

Page _____

No.   Answer

___ _____
___ _____
___ _____
___ _____
___ _____
___ _____
___ _____
___ _____
___ _____
___ _____
___ _____
___ _____
___ _____
___ _____
___ _____
___ _____
___ _____
___ _____
___ _____
___ _____
___ _____
___ _____
___ _____
___ _____
___ _____
___ _____
___ _____
___ _____
___ _____

Name _____

Class Hour _____

Page _____

No.   Answer

___ _____
___ _____
___ _____
___ _____
___ _____
___ _____
___ _____
___ _____
___ _____
___ _____
___ _____
___ _____
___ _____
___ _____
___ _____
___ _____
___ _____
___ _____
___ _____
___ _____
___ _____
___ _____
___ _____
___ _____
___ _____
___ _____
___ _____
___ _____
___ _____

Name	
Class Hour	
Page	
No.	Answer

Name	
Class Hour	
Page	
No.	Answer

Name	
Class Hour	
Page	
No.	Answer

Name			Name			Name	
Class Hour			Class Hour			Class Hour	
Page			Page			Page	
No.	Answer		No.	Answer		No.	Answer

Name _____

Class Hour _____

Page _____

No.   Answer

_____ _____
_____ _____
_____ _____
_____ _____
_____ _____
_____ _____
_____ _____
_____ _____
_____ _____
_____ _____
_____ _____
_____ _____
_____ _____
_____ _____
_____ _____
_____ _____
_____ _____
_____ _____
_____ _____
_____ _____
_____ _____
_____ _____
_____ _____
_____ _____
_____ _____
_____ _____
_____ _____
_____ _____
_____ _____
_____ _____

Name _____

Class Hour _____

Page _____

No.   Answer

_____ _____
_____ _____
_____ _____
_____ _____
_____ _____
_____ _____
_____ _____
_____ _____
_____ _____
_____ _____
_____ _____
_____ _____
_____ _____
_____ _____
_____ _____
_____ _____
_____ _____
_____ _____
_____ _____
_____ _____
_____ _____
_____ _____
_____ _____
_____ _____
_____ _____
_____ _____
_____ _____
_____ _____
_____ _____
_____ _____

Name _____

Class Hour _____

Page _____

No.   Answer

_____ _____
_____ _____
_____ _____
_____ _____
_____ _____
_____ _____
_____ _____
_____ _____
_____ _____
_____ _____
_____ _____
_____ _____
_____ _____
_____ _____
_____ _____
_____ _____
_____ _____
_____ _____
_____ _____
_____ _____
_____ _____
_____ _____
_____ _____
_____ _____
_____ _____
_____ _____
_____ _____
_____ _____
_____ _____
_____ _____

Name		Name		Name	
Class Hour		Class Hour		Class Hour	
Page		Page		Page	
No.	Answer	No.	Answer	No.	Answer

Name _____

Class Hour _____

Page _____

No.   Answer

_____ _____
_____ _____
_____ _____
_____ _____
_____ _____
_____ _____
_____ _____
_____ _____
_____ _____
_____ _____
_____ _____
_____ _____
_____ _____
_____ _____
_____ _____
_____ _____
_____ _____
_____ _____
_____ _____
_____ _____
_____ _____
_____ _____
_____ _____
_____ _____
_____ _____
_____ _____
_____ _____
_____ _____
_____ _____
_____ _____
_____ _____
_____ _____
_____ _____
_____ _____
_____ _____

Name _____

Class Hour _____

Page _____

No.   Answer

_____ _____
_____ _____
_____ _____
_____ _____
_____ _____
_____ _____
_____ _____
_____ _____
_____ _____
_____ _____
_____ _____
_____ _____
_____ _____
_____ _____
_____ _____
_____ _____
_____ _____
_____ _____
_____ _____
_____ _____
_____ _____
_____ _____
_____ _____
_____ _____
_____ _____
_____ _____
_____ _____
_____ _____
_____ _____
_____ _____
_____ _____
_____ _____
_____ _____
_____ _____
_____ _____

Name _____

Class Hour _____

Page _____

No.   Answer

_____ _____
_____ _____
_____ _____
_____ _____
_____ _____
_____ _____
_____ _____
_____ _____
_____ _____
_____ _____
_____ _____
_____ _____
_____ _____
_____ _____
_____ _____
_____ _____
_____ _____
_____ _____
_____ _____
_____ _____
_____ _____
_____ _____
_____ _____
_____ _____
_____ _____
_____ _____
_____ _____
_____ _____
_____ _____
_____ _____
_____ _____
_____ _____
_____ _____
_____ _____
_____ _____